# Questions about God

**A guide for A/AS Level students**

Patrick J. Clarke

Stanley Thornes (Publishers) Ltd

Text © Patrick J. Clarke 1999

Original line illustrations © Stanley Thornes (Publishers) Ltd 1999

The right of Patrick J. Clarke to be identified as author of this work has been asserted by him in accordance with the Copyright, Designs and Patents Act 1988.

All rights reserved. No part of this publication may be reproduced or transmitted in any form or by any means, electronic or mechanical, including photocopy, recording or any information storage and retrieval system, without permission in writing from the publisher or under licence from the Copyright Licensing Agency Limited. Further details of such licences (for reprographic reproduction) may be obtained from the Copyright Licensing Agency Limited, of 90 Tottenham Court Road, London W1P 0LP.

First published in 1999 by:
Stanley Thornes (Publishers) Ltd
Ellenborough House
Wellington Street
CHELTENHAM GL50 1YW
England

99 00 01 02 03 / 10 9 8 7 6 5 4 3 2 1

A catalogue record for this book is available from the British Library.

ISBN 0-7487-4340-5

Typeset by Wyvern 21, Bristol
Illustrated by Angela Lumley
Cover design by Mike Cryer
Edited by Geoffrey D. Palmer

Printed and bound in Great Britain by T. J. International Ltd., Padstow, Cornwall

**Acknowledgements**
The line illustrations in this book have been redrawn from originals created by the author.

With thanks to the following for permission to reproduce photographs in this book:
Patrick J. Clarke, pages 93, 108, 141;
Mary Evans Picture Library, pages 48, 52, 113, 121;
Hulton Getty, pages 14, 153;
Scala, Florence, page 154.

Every effort has been made to contact copyright holders. The publishers apologise to anyone whose rights have been inadvertently overlooked, and will be happy to rectify any errors or omissions.

*Author's note*
I dedicate this book to my family in England and in Ireland, and to all the friends I have met on the way – in Carlow College; in Old Leeds; at St Bede's Grammar School, Bradford; in the C.M.S. in London; at Louvain University; at Trinity and All Saints Colleges; at Lancaster University; and at Mayfield College in Sussex – and to the students of Bishop Challoner, Shortlands, South London, whose interest in theology played no small part in the creation of this book.

# Contents

**About this Book**     v

**Complementary Reading**     vi

**1 The Existence and Nature of God**     1

    I The study of God     1
*Natural theology* 1 – *Revealed theology* 2 – *The idea of God in Christian theology* 3 – *The truths of revelation* 5 – *A new understanding of revelation* 5 – *Faith* 10 – *The attributes of God* 16 – *Other divine attributes* 19

    II Arguments for God's existence     23
*Anselm: the ontological argument* 23 – *Criticisms of the ontological argument* 26 – *The cosmological argument* 28 – *The Five Ways of St Thomas Aquinas* 30 – *The cosmological argument: other thinkers* 31 – *The teleological argument* 33 – *The Enlightenment critique of natural theology* 35 – *The moral argument for God's existence* 37 – *Kant's moral argument* 38 – *Updating the arguments* 40 – *The cumulative case argument* 43

**2 God and Science**     45

    I The growing influence of science     45
*The medieval world view* 45 – *Copernicus and Galileo* 46 – *Isaac Newton (1642–1727)* 49 – *Implications for natural theology* 49

    II The challenge of modern science     51
*The theory of evolution* 53 – *Evolution and the Bible* 54 – *Reactions to Darwin* 57 – *Positive responses to evolution* 59 – *The challenge of cosmology* 61 – *The science of history* 63 – *Negative responses to modern science* 65

III Science and religion: can they be reconciled? 68
*Some preliminary issues: different causalities* 68 – *The responses of modern theologians* 70 – *Differing perspectives* 77 – *Changes in the scientific landscape: quantum physics* 80 – *Advances in science: what theology has learned* 82 – *Theology since evolution* 85

## 3 God and Experience 89

I Religious experience: direct and indirect 92
*Conversion experiences* 94 – *Mystical experience* 98 – *Assessment of religious experience* 103 – *Problems of religious experience* 104 – *Indirect religious experience* 107 – *Miracles* 109

II Interpreting experience: theism or atheism 112
*F. D. E. Schleiermacher (1768–1834)* 112 – *Ludwig Feuerbach (1804–1872)* 114 – *The influence of Feuerbach* 115

III The problem of evil 125
*The Augustinian theodicy* 126 – *The Irenaean theodicy* 128 – *New Testament theodicy* 130 – *The choice: faith or atheism* 131 – *A summary of the problem* 133

## 4 God and Language 135

I Speaking about God 136
*The way of analogy* 136 – *Symbolic language* 139 – *Myth* 141 – *Justifying religious language* 142

II The challenge of logical positivism 143
*Verification and falsification* 144 – *Responses to logical positivism* 147 – *The roots of religious language: the mystical* 151 – *Ludwig Wittgenstein (1889–1951)* 152 – *Religion as cognitive* 156

III New ideas of God 158
*Rudolf Bultmann (1884–1976)* 160 – *John Macquarrie* 162 – *Paul Tillich (1896–1965)* 164 – *Dietrich Bonhoeffer (1906–1945)* 165 – *Don Cupitt* 167 – *Process theology* 168

## Answering Examination Questions 173

## Glossary 181

## Index 193

# About this Book

This book is essentially a work of philosophical theology. This is to say that it deals with theological questions in the light of the challenge posed by philosophy, in four key areas. Chapter 1 deals with the Christian understanding of God, and the modern rationalist challenge to the question of God's existence. Chapter 2 is concerned with the modern challenge of science to religious faith. Chapter 3 is concerned with religious experience, and examines the challenge to its credibility from the rise of atheistic interpretations that have owed a lot to the development of the social sciences. Chapter 4 looks at the way in which religious language is used, and how this language is exposed to empiricist theories that seek to undermine its validity and meaningfulness.

Although the book is divided into four chapters, these chapters are not independent of each other. Students will be able to see points of contact between them. For instance, the challenge of science already appears in Chapter 1, and later in Chapter 4; theological proposals in Chapter 1 appear again in Chapter 4; and Chapters 3 and 4 overlap for logical and theological reasons.

The names of authors are generally in **bold type** to aid memory. Diagrams, illustrations and some additional material are added here and there to function as summaries, trigger discussion, raise questions or provide food for thought.

While the book is on the universal subject of God, for reasons of scholarship – among others – it is written from within the context of the Western Christian tradition.

This book does not claim to be comprehensive. The hope is that students will be stimulated by it to pursue further study in many of the areas covered. It is also hoped that by reading it, students will gain an insight into the relevance of theology – and of its close companion, philosophy – to the problems and questions of modern life.

# Complementary Reading

This book makes frequent reference to the writings of many theologians and philosophers. As you read and study further, you may find it useful to consult some of the following works.

Brooke, J. H. (1991) *Science and Religion: Some Historical Perspectives*. Cambridge: Cambridge University Press.
Buber, M. (1923) *I and Thou*. London.
Cosslett, T. (ed.) (1984) *Science and Religion in the Nineteenth Century*. Cambridge: Cambridge University Press.
Freud, S. (1962) *The Future of an Illusion*. London: Hogarth.
Hick, J. (1963) *Philosophy of Religion*. Englewood Cliffs, NJ: Prentice-Hall.
Hick, J. (1966) *Evil and the God of Love*. London: Macmillan.
Hooykaas, R. (1973) *Religion and the Rise of Modern Science*. Edinburgh: Scottish Academic Press.
James, W. (1945) *The Varieties of Religious Experience*. London: Longman.
Kenny, A. (1972) *Does God Exist?* London.
Kerr, F. (1986) *Theology after Wittgenstein*. Oxford: Blackwell.
Kung, H. (1980) *Does God Exist?: an Answer for Today*. London: Collins.
Macquarrie, J. (1955) *An Existentialist Theology: a Comparison of Heidegger and Bultmann*. London: S.C.M. Press.
Macquarrie, J. (1966) *Principles of Christian Theology*. London: S.C.M. Press.
Martin, J. A. (1966) *The New Dialogue Between Philosophy and Theology*. London: Black.
McGinn, B. (1992) *The Foundations of Mysticism*. London: SCM.
McGrath, A. E. (ed.) (1993) *The Blackwell Encyclopedia of Modern Christian Thought*. Oxford: Blackwell.
Owen, H. P. (1971) *Concepts of Deity*. London: Macmillan.
Polkinghorne, J. C. (1988) *Science and Creation: the Search for Understanding*. London: SPCK.
Richardson, A. (ed.) (1969) *A Dictionary of Christian Theology*. London: S.C.M. Press.
Richmond, J. (1970) *Theology and Metaphysics*. London: S.C.M. Press.
Schleiermacher, F. D. E. (1958) *On Religion: Speeches to its Cultured Despisers*. New York: Harper & Row.
Scruton, R. (1990) *The Philosopher on Dover Beach: Essays*. Manchester: Carcanet.
Swinburne, R. (1977) *The Coherence of Theism*. Oxford: Clarendon Press.
Swinburne, R. (1996) *Is there a God?* Oxford: Oxford University Press.
Wakefield, G. S. (ed.) (1983) *A Dictionary of Christian Spirituality*. London: SCM.
Ward, K. (1974) *The Concept of God*. Oxford: Blackwell.
Wilkes, K. (1969) *The Rise of Modern Science*. Oxford.

# Chapter 1 | The Existence and Nature of God

## 1 THE STUDY OF GOD

The study of God is properly called *theology* (from the Greek words *theos*, meaning 'God', and *logos*, 'study of', or 'words about'). In its earliest form, it meant the study of the scriptures. One of the great theologians of the early medieval period, **Peter Abelard** (1079–1142), broadened the meaning of theology to include the philosophical treatment of Christian doctrines. By the time of **Thomas Aquinas** (1226–1274), theology had become divided into *revealed* theology and *natural* theology.

## Natural theology

Natural theology is the enterprise of seeking knowledge of God's existence by the use of reason alone. **Aquinas's** *Five Ways* of proving God's existence came to be seen as the classic example of natural theology. The first reference to what is now called natural theology is probably by **St Paul** in Rom. 1.20: 'For since the creation of the world God's invisible qualities – his eternal power and divine nature – have been clearly seen, being understood from what has been made …'.

The early Christian thinker **Tertullian** (AD 160–220) was opposed to mixing faith and reason, and therefore was against natural theology. In a memorable phrase, he said that Jerusalem (the centre of faith) owed nothing to Athens (the centre of reason). **Pascal** also strongly objected to natural theology. He believed that it only yielded a pale shadow of the true God. In a famous expression, he distinguished between the *God of the Philosophers* and the *God of the Theologians*, the latter being the God of the Bible, accessible only through faith.

**Aquinas**, on the other hand, had a positive attitude to reason. He believed that through natural theology it was possible to know of God's existence, and some things about His nature. For instance, God cannot be a contingent being like us; that is, a being whose existence depends on some prior cause. God's essence is to exist, which is to say that His essence and existence are identical. Another way of putting this is to say that God is a necessary being. While Aquinas made natural theology an explicit category in its own right, he was not the first theologian to use reason to speak of God's existence and nature. **Anselm of Canterbury** (1033–1109) had earlier defined God as 'that than which nothing greater can be conceived'. He also declared that he couldn't think of God as not existing, thus anticipating Aquinas. In 1870, in a bold move, the Vatican Council declared that the existence of God can be known by the light of reason alone. In what sense and to what extent God's existence can be known by the light of reason is a matter of dispute.

Both Anselm and Aquinas were already believers in God before they made any attempt to use reason. It is more likely that both saw God's existence as something which could be shown to be consistent with reason, rather than something that could be established by reason alone. Whether it is theoretically true that God's existence can be known by reason may be argued, but it is beyond dispute that, as a fact of life, reason alone does not normally yield knowledge of God. This point has been defended both theologically and philosophically.

Natural theology can also speak about what God must be like as a matter of logical necessity. For instance, God must be without any limitations. This means that He must be infinite. Any being with limitations could not claim to be God. God must also be eternal, having no beginning and no end. This is another way of saying that God is a necessary being, as we saw above. Again, the notion of God means the absence of any rival 'god'. This is to say that there can only be one God, since the idea of many gods is self-contradictory.

But, as Aquinas said, natural theology cannot tell us very much about God. To know about the God of the Christian faith, it is necessary to rely on the *revelation* which God has made of Himself. This takes us to revealed theology.

## Revealed theology

Aquinas saw natural theology as laying a foundation for revealed theology. In revealed theology, we come to know truths that God has revealed about Himself. The main source of revealed theology is the Bible. In revealed theology, the key truths of the Christian faith come to be known. These include the doctrines of creation, the Trinity, the Incarnation and the Atonement. It needs to be mentioned, however, that the understanding of revealed theology is not cut and dried. In modern times, many of the presuppositions of God's revelation have come under question (see below, Revelation). One of these is the nature of the Bible itself, the foundation of revealed theology. Modern biblical scholarship has brought about a new understanding of the Bible as a divinely inspired book. Its human character is now much better understood. One effect of this is to create a new understanding of revelation. Far from being a matter of *truths* being revealed, revelation is now seen as an interpersonal communication in which man comes to apprehend the reality of God. Even the so-called 'truths of revelation' are themselves the constant subject of study. The examination of faith in the sense of the truths of revelation has always been an essential part of theology. This was put succinctly by **St Augustine** (AD 354–430), when he defined theology as 'faith seeking understanding'.

## Theology

| Natural | Revealed |
|---|---|
| Based on reason (which includes human experience) | Based on prior faith in God and on the acceptance of the Bible as the record of God's revelation |

*Why is this distinction unsatisfactory today (see p. 7)?*

## The idea of God in Christian theology

The Christian understanding of God is essentially derived from the Bible. In the Bible, God reveals Himself as a supernatural being who communicates with man. In this communication, God essentially reveals His will (1 Tim. 2.4) and his law (Exod. 20.1–21). Further revelations of God's will recur throughout the Old Testament, especially in the prophetic literature.

In the New Testament, God communicates 'through his Son' (Heb. 1.2). It was because God 'so loved the world that he sent his Son that those who believed in him might not perish but have eternal life' (John 3.16).

## Questions about God

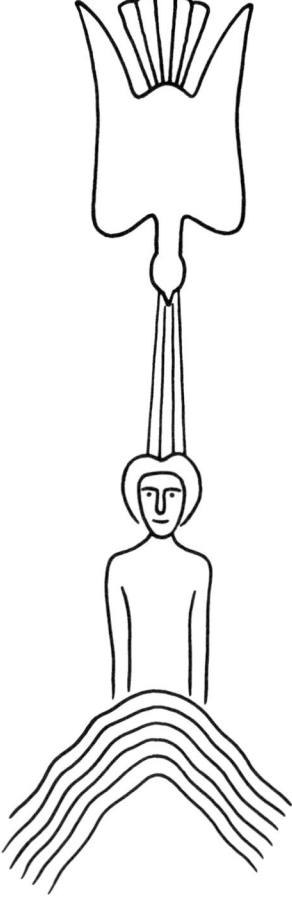

The Trinity, from a Gospels cover, c. 900–980, in the Staatbibliothek, Munich. The Trinity is an example of revealed theology. Aquinas said it could never be discovered by reason. This illustration shows the baptism of Jesus (Mark 1.10–11)

The God revealed in the Bible is also a triune God. In traditional theology creation is attributed to the Father, redemption to the Son and sanctification to the Holy Spirit. How the three Persons are distinct and yet equal in sharing the one divine nature is regarded as a truth of revelation beyond normal understanding.

## The truths of revelation

Aquinas considered revelation to be essentially a source of truths about God which we could never know by reason alone. Central among these truths was the Trinity and the story of redemption. This understanding of revelation in terms of *truths* was to play a major part in the events that led to the splitting of the Church at the Reformation. Where the truths of revelation were 'contained' was a big issue for both sides. On the Catholic side, it was claimed that the truths were contained in 'scripture and tradition'. The reformers insisted on the principle of 'scripture alone'. This was to enable the reformers to justify jettisoning Church customs that had no apparent scriptural basis, and ultimately to justify the Reformation itself. In any case, both sides were locked in a struggle for 'truth' or 'truths' that were supposed to be contained in either scripture or tradition. This came to be called the *propositional* view of revelation.

## A new understanding of revelation

The old understanding of revelation was based on an unhistorical view of the Bible. With the introduction of the *historical–critical method* of interpreting the Bible in the seventeenth century, there came a new appreciation of the human character of biblical literature. No longer was it possible to treat the Bible as a book of divine oracles, delivered once by God and faithfully recorded by its authors through divine inspiration. It was now realised that the biblical authors were products of their time, and their understanding of divine truth was understood in such a way that it was culturally conditioned. But even more important was the realisation that their basic message was, first and foremost, the outcome of an *experience*. As **Karl Rahner**, in *Theological Investigations* (1961), put it, 'It may be supposed that the apostles themselves had a global experience [of Christ] ... lying behind propositions ... and forming a source for the articulation of the faith in propositions.' This meant that a distinction needed to be made between expressions of truth and the underlying *experience of God* (or Christ) from which the later truths emerged. In other words, there was a new awareness of revelation as primarily an experience of God. Only later was it codified into a message, or body, of truths. This is known as the *non-propositional* view of revelation.

*Revelation as experience*
The emergence of the non-propositional view of revelation was a reaction to the polemics of the post-Reformation period, that had stressed the external *message* of revelation. This had resulted in the message becoming detached from its proper source, God. Christian apologetics, especially in the form of religious education in schools, had become arid and lifeless, centring on a list of facts about God and Christ that had become uninspiring. This was a view strongly held by the American theologian **Gabriel Moran**. In his *Theology of Revelation* (1967), Moran argued that revelation was essentially linked to the experience of God, a view only recognised by the **Vatican Council** a short time before. In Moran's words, revelation is 'a personal communion of knowledge, an interrelationship of God and the individual within a believing community'. For Moran, revelation is the self-disclosure of God by way of a personal relationship. The classic example was the person of Christ, who lies at the centre of all revelation. It was through Christ as a person that the truth about God was finally revealed. Only in the context of an interpersonal relationship, now as then, can any truth about God be meaningful.

In this view creeds, dogmas and teachings are not to be identified with revelation. By themselves they are merely things – objects – with no power to inspire. But seen as part of a human relationship with God through other people, they become revelatory. The part played by other people in making revelation happen is something of a major key in Moran's thought. It follows from his stress on the person of Christ as the medium of God's revelation to mankind.

Other theologians have seen revelation as something possible within ordinary human life, but have nevertheless seen it as an experience.

The German theologian **Schleiermacher** saw revelation as the experience of God that was perceptible in the feeling and intuition of *dependence* (see also Chapter 3). He distinguished between this experience, which lies at the root of religion, and *ideas* about God, which take the form of truths and dogmas. More recently, the psychologist **Carl Jung** has made a similar distinction. He saw the therapeutic value of religious faith in the power of religious experience, not in external adherence to the dogmas and teachings of the Church.

**John Macquarrie** is another modern writer who sees revelation to be primarily about experience. In *Principles of Christian Theology* (1966), he describes revelation as the gracious in-breaking of the divine, or holy into human consciousness. 'Revelation is not primarily given in the form of statements ... that which discloses itself in revelation seizes the whole being of man and cannot be adequately expressed within the limits of language.' However, Macquarrie distinguishes between what he calls the *classic* or *primordial* revelation on which communities of faith are founded, and the subsequent reflection on it by believers. He calls the latter *repetitive* revelation. Once again, we see a clear recognition of the relationship between the message of revelation and its underlying source in the being of God.

These theologians have raised the question as to whether the distinction between revealed and natural theology is any longer a satisfactory one. The question follows from the fact that revelation of a fundamental kind is already available within human nature. One solution to this is to recognise that all revelation is assisted by grace and comes from God. In this view, the Christian faith is seen as an instance of *special* revelation.

## Understanding revelation

| | |
|---|---|
| Faith | Assent to revelation |
| Scripture | Medium of revelation |
| Theology | Reflection on revelation |

*How has the modern understanding of revelation changed these definitions?*

However, some theologians have stressed the traditional *content* of revelation as the message of God's love for mankind. This emerges clearly in the writings of **Søren Kierkegaard** (1813–1855), who saw revelation as the story of God's redemptive plans for man in Jesus Christ. Although Kierkegaard notoriously stressed the subjective appropriation of the Christian message in the personal leap of faith, as opposed to the blandness of objective Church membership, he did not lose sight of its objective *significance*. In reaction to **Hegel**, who had seen Christianity as the working out of a necessary cosmic system, Kierkegaard highlighted its *unlikely* and *undeserved* character. The Christian message could never be humanly predicted: it is the 'absolute paradox' involving God becoming man in a free act of love. But for Kierkegaard it was the Christian *message* that was to be inwardly appropriated in faith.

This aspect of revelation has been firmly underlined in the twentieth century in the writings of **Karl Barth** (1886–1968). Barth reacted strongly against the humanistic so-called 'liberal theology' represented by Schleiermacher, in which the emphasis was placed on man the recipient rather than on God the gracious revealer. For Barth, God's gracious revelation contained in the Bible and the preaching of the Church must be given absolute priority. It is addressed to man, and invites a gracious response of faith and gratitude.

It must also be said, however, that those theologians who have stressed the message of revelation have not intended it to be treated as an *object* or a *thing*. They too have wanted to stress the *personal* aspect of God's self-giving. To borrow the language of **Martin Buber**, in his book *I and Thou* (1923), they have wanted revelation to be seen as an *I–Thou* encounter; in other words, an encounter with another person. This is of a different order to an *I–It* encounter, which reduces the 'You' to an 'It', and turns the encounter into an objective relationship with a 'thing'. God can never be a thing.

## Aspects of revelation

**Propositional**
Revelation is the sum of truths and doctrines contained either in scripture or tradition – it is said to lead to an *I–It* relationship if misunderstood

**Non-propositional**
Revelation is an experience of God which comes prior to truths – the experience is linked to a personal (*I–You*) relationship with God

*To what extent does Buber provide the key for understanding the two aspects of revelation? How can the two aspects be harmonised?*

## The possibility of revelation

The question of the possibility of revelation is one that has engaged some modern theologians. The move is to show how the idea of a revelation from God can be seen to answer certain needs within the human condition. In this approach, man is seen as the 'question' to which God is the 'answer'. This makes it possible to set revelation within a philosophical context; that is, within the nature of man.

This approach underlies the existential thought of **Rudolf Bultmann** (see Chapter 4). For Bultmann, the Christian message is the answer to man's striving for authentic existence, and offers him the possibility of achieving it.

The Protestant theologian **Paul Tillich** (see Chapter 4), in *Reason and Revelation* (1951), argues that aspects of human experience (such as contingence and mortality) raise the question of man's dependence on a source external to himself. The Christian revelation can then be seen as the answer that man is waiting for. The Catholic theologian **Karl Rahner**, in *Hearers of the Word* (1941), argues along similar lines, using the notion of human *transcendence*. Because we are never satisfied with any state we reach, or any knowledge we may possess, we have to recognise the fact that we are always wanting to go beyond where we are. This is transcendence, a function of the human spirit, and it is only ultimately satisfied by God. The Christian revelation is the promise that our endless striving will eventually be fulfilled.

This idea is also taken up by **John Macquarrie** (see also Chapter 4). He believes that God is perceived in our human awareness of finitude and anxiety. This means our inability to realise our full potential as human beings, causing us concern and *Angst*. He says, 'We can, I believe, trace something like a coherent pattern of experience that leads from man's questioning of his own existence to the religious confrontation with holy being ...'. God's revelation is thus seen as an answer to the existential frustration that characterises our life in the world.

*Questions about God*

# Revelation and human existence

| Answer | Questions |
|---|---|
| God's self-revelation is an answer to man's sense of his limitations and is an offer of their fulfilment | Finitude, transcendence, anxiety, fallenness, dependence, mystery, openness |

*Does revelation answer man's existential needs?*
*What might an atheist say?*

*Summary*
The old understanding of revelation was dominated by concerns with truth and error. This led to an over-preoccupation with the idea that revelation was captured in truths and propositions. This has now been replaced by an awareness of the interpersonal character of revelation as a communication of God to man. This means that revelation is primarily an interpersonal experience in which God is known. Only when this happens are the 'truths' of revelation able to make sense. The fundamental idea of revelation is to be understood as the divine answer to man's existential needs, in terms of an *I–You* relationship between man and God.

## Faith

The meaning of faith has been a contentious issue in the history of Christian thought. In the Catholic tradition, faith has tended to be identified with the *content* of what is believed. In this sense, faith becomes closely identified with revelation seen as truths and dogmas.

Traditionally, this has been known as *fides quae* (faith in terms of its object). In the Protestant tradition following the Reformation, faith came to be identified with an attitude of *trust* in God through Christ. This put the emphasis on the subjective response to the object of faith. This subjective aspect of faith became known as the *fides qua*. One effect of the Reformation was to lead to a hardening of attitudes on both sides about the content of faith. Central to the debate was the issue of the 'sources' of faith. Was it scripture alone, as the Reformers held, or did it also include the traditions of the Church, as the Catholics insisted? This preoccupation has now given way to a more personal understanding of faith as a relationship to God, which includes hope and charity.

## Faith and knowledge

In the modern period, faith has begun to be contrasted with knowledge. Under the influence of positivism, knowledge has tended to be confined to what can be scientifically ascertained by experience and empirical verification. By contrast, faith has been cast as a second-rate claim to knowledge, which lacks justification for lack of empirical evidence.

Reactions to this have usually been to argue that faith is a reasonable response to given data. This can take the form of either arguing that there are solid reasons for faith (evidentialism) or arguing that faith provides its own justification (fideism). The traditional Catholic approach includes the appeal to the credibility of the Church as an organisation which puts its weight behind the claims of faith and guarantees its authenticity. Individual Catholic theologians such as **Karl Rahner** have argued on the basis of man's make-up that faith is a critical answer to man's search for meaning and is therefore a reasonable human response. The modern Lutheran theologian **Wolfhart Pannenberg** believes that faith can be grounded on solid historical evidence visible to everyone, based on the Resurrection, but still leaves room for trust (*fiducia*) that God will be faithful to His promises now and in the future, because Christ the man has been raised.

A more typically Protestant approach is taken by **Søren Kierkegaard**, who argued in *Philosophical Fragments* (1844) that faith (in Christ) requires an unsupported *leap* into the unknown. This daring *leap of faith* leads to the knowledge that is essential to make sense of life, and provides the enlightenment that man is looking for. While Kierkegaard's approach may be termed *fideistic* and to some extent irrational, he would argue that in the end it is an existentially justified move. In this sense, it is 'reasonable'.

Some of these ideas will surface again in our next section, on faith and reason.

## Questions about God

# Faith

Tertullian    Augustine    Anselm    Aquinas
  Pascal         Luther
  Kierkegaard    Bultmann         Barth
Pannenberg                                Rahner

*How can these names be grouped for similarities and differences?*

*Faith and reason*
The need to make faith intelligible already calls for the use of reason. The earliest statements of faith in the Creeds employed ideas taken from Greek philosophy. An example of this was the attempt to explain how Christ could be human *and* divine, which involved the philosophical problem of explaining how two natures could subsist in one person.

The relationship between faith and reason became a contentious issue at the Reformation. The use of reason was seen to contaminate the purity of faith by making use of a man-made foundation to make faith secure, thus turning it into a 'work'. This would detract from its nature as a grace of God. **Martin Luther** argued that faith, if it is to be a meritorious and saving act, must be a free act, devoid of any security. Besides, he saw reason as a human faculty corrupted by the Fall and therefore it could provide no true knowledge of God. Luther was here echoing **St Augustine**, who had seen faith as prior to reason as the way to truth. As he famously put it, 'I believe in order to understand.'

# The origin of faith

*In what sense are all three related? Are the arrows pointing correctly? Is the sequence correct?*

## The Existence and Nature of God

A different approach had been taken by **Thomas Aquinas**. He saw reason as a God-given faculty that enabled man to have a rudimentary knowledge of God's existence. But reason could only take man a certain distance. To know God fully, it was necessary to believe the truths of revelation revolving round the story of redemption. These truths were to become the object of faith. Aquinas also believed it was important to be able to show that faith is not irrational. It is a matter of debate whether his *Five Ways* were really meant for believers who already possessed faith, or for unbelievers who might be persuaded to come to faith. In either case, his arguments were aimed to show that faith was highly consistent with reason.

However, it would be unfair to accuse Aquinas of relying on reason. In his definition of faith he said that it was an act which rested ultimately on the 'authority of God who reveals'. Here Aquinas anticipates the Reformers by showing that faith involves the act of *trust*. But there is at least a difference of emphasis between the thought of Aquinas and that of Luther. This can be seen in the very negative assessment of reason shown by **Kierkegaard**, who followed in the Lutheran tradition. He regarded reason as an obstacle to faith. Reason only leads down blind alleys. Reasonable people would never make sense of the truths of faith. The cold logic of Athens would make little sense of the paradoxical happenings in Jerusalem. Reason is active human searching; faith is a decision to surrender to the truth of God. These differing views about the nature of faith continue to keep alive the debate about faith and reason.

## *Faith and reason*

| Aquinas *et al*. | Augustine *et al*. |
|---|---|
| Reason supports faith by showing that faith is a reasonable interpretation of the world. Faith also offers an answer to the problems of human existence | Faith comes before reason and shows us the true meaning of life. Reason can never lead to faith. Faith must be an option freely taken in trust |

*To what extent does this illustrate the relationship between faith and reason? Is faith ever irrational?*

Søren Kierkegaard stressed the subjective inwardness of faith. How has he influenced the new ideas of God (see Chapter 4)?

## Pascal's Wager

An interesting contribution to the debate about faith and reason has been made by the enigmatic French mathematician and religious thinker **Blaise Pascal** (1623–1662). Pascal had little time for **Descartes'** preoccupation with intellectual certainty. This was something he considered unrealistic in the light of the existential uncertainty that haunts man in his everyday life. Man has a problem coping with this everyday uncertainty. It is not solved by the Cartesian method of trying to arrive at watertight rational truth. In real life, this is an impossible quest. In the real world, man is beset with irrational tendencies and emotions, such as prejudice, pride, passion and bias. With such things always interfering with his view, man can never arrive at a clear vision of the truth. Indeed, it is doubtful if man very often *cares* about the truth. You only need to look at the lawyer, said Pascal, who cares more about his fee and winning his case than he does about real justice. Great men are usually more worried about catching hares and winning at the races than they are about the niceties of philosophical truth!

Given all this, is it not more realistic to take a practical approach and face the fact that life will always be clouded by doubt and uncertainty? Pascal's approach was to propose making a wager. Why not listen to those who say that life is a test that leads to a great loss or a great reward? Those who in the end are found worthy are in for an eternity of bliss. Those who fail the test are destined for an eternity of damnation. That, in fact, is the message preached by Jesus Christ. Therefore, why not go for the gamble and aim for the lifestyle most likely to lead to the passing of the test? Here is the essence of Pascal's Wager. Not to opt for the right lifestyle is to gamble with eternity.

The outlay is a relatively short life, whereas the prize is eternal. If the gamble comes off, the prize was worth it. If the gamble does not come off, very little is lost. On the other hand, to risk living a dissolute life is a stupid gamble, and those who live as if there was no eternity may be in for a nasty shock. A short span of dissolute living may end in an eternity of torment.

To be fair to Pascal, he did not himself see faith as a gamble. He was a deeply religious man, who was merely trying to show the implications of faith to his unbelieving contemporaries. He knew that reason was no path to religious faith. The only choice left was to take a sensible risk and to wager one's life by following the way laid down by Jesus Christ. For Pascal, this was the smart way to bet.

But even faith, Pascal warned, can be infected with rational preoccupations. There can be no escaping the risk factor. Some seek security by relying on authority, whether the Bible or the Church. This is a mistake, because such reliance is a seeking after foolproof grounds for trust. After all, the ancients had no such authority to fall back on. Faith, as **St Augustine** had held, is a decision of the *will*. For Pascal, a humble sense of sin was essential before taking the decision. Looking for proofs of God without a sense of sin leads to pride. But a sense of sin without faith in God leads to despair. In both cases, God is being short-changed. In the former, faith is flawed by looking for too much proof. In the latter, it is flawed by too much doubt. For Pascal, the secret lay in trusting the instincts of the heart. As he famously said, 'The heart has reasons the mind never thought of.'

Clearly, Pascal saw faith in *ethical* terms as the expression of a good will. For this reason, he may be said to anticipate **Kant**, who linked faith with moral duty – and also modern thinkers such as **Bultmann**, who saw faith in terms of authentic existence, and **Karl Rahner**, who saw faith as identical with personal moral integrity.

## Pascal's two views of God

| Philosophers | Theologians |
| --- | --- |
| Prime mover, first cause, necessary being, eternal, perfect, infinite, one | Three in one, loving, forgiving, redeeming, guiding, giving, saving, calling |
| Deduced from reason and logic. Rejected by Pascal and Luther | Revealed in the Bible and through Jesus Christ |

*Which one did Pascal criticise, and why? Is Pascal's distinction valid?*

## The attributes of God

*Omnipotence*
The word 'omnipotent' comes from the Latin, meaning 'all-powerful' or 'almighty'. This attribute is affirmed by the Old Testament: 'I know that you are all powerful' (Job 42.2). 'With God all things are possible', said Jesus (Matt. 19.26).

**Anthony Kenny**, in *The God of the Philosophers* (1989), said that God's omnipotence means His sovereignty, His rule and overall control. He points out how the ancient Greeks such as Xenophon had speculated on whether God could do what was logically impossible. In the Christian tradition, this is ruled out. The idea that God acts out of necessity has been a cause of difficulty. For instance, **Aquinas** agreed with **Abelard** that God couldn't sin (of necessity), yet Abelard was condemned at the Council of Sens (1140) for concluding from this that God is somehow limited in how He acts. **John Wycliffe** was similarly condemned at the Council of Constance (1414) for saying that God couldn't have created a better world because He acts out of necessity.

**Descartes** held that God has no limits in respect of what is logically possible. **Leibniz** held that God was always constrained by His wisdom and always acts according to its dictates. For this reason, God created the best of all possible worlds for the achievement of His purposes. However, only God knows this.

In recent times **Richard Swinburne**, in *The Coherence of Theism* (1977), appears to agree with Leibniz. He rightly argues that it is no limitation on God's part that He always acts freely and rationally. This is only to say that, paradoxically, He *necessarily* acts freely and rationally. This in turn means that He cannot do what would be evil or irrational, but that is not a limitation! A God who could act against His wisdom by doing what was evil or irrational would not be worthy of our adoration or worship.

*Omnipotence and free will*
The attribute of God's omnipotence is thrown into relief by two things. One is the fact of evil and suffering. How can God claim to be good and omnipotent in the light of all the evil and suffering in the world? A more extensive treatment of this question is carried out in Chapter 3 (see discussion of *theodicies*), but for the moment the classical answer is that God does not interfere in the world because it would mean taking away the gift of our free will. **Thomas Tracy** (1984) believes that God alters his omnipotence to allow for human free will: 'God limits the scope of his power on purpose to give humans freedom. This does not contradict God's omnipotence, only defines its use.' **Maurice Wiles** (1986) agrees: 'It is God's will to manifest his power by the creation of free beings.' **Keith Ward** (1982) makes a similar point: 'God freely limits the exercise of his unlimited power by the creation of free beings.' **Grace Jantzen** (1980) adds a further point: 'God's power is to give autonomy to his creatures out of love. God's love is central: other attributes are subordinate to it.' A similar view had already been expressed by Kierkegaard when he said, 'God's omnipotence is always under the power of his love.' In 'process theology' (see Chapter 4) God's omnipotence is clearly con-

strained by the actions of human beings, and is to some extent dependent on them.

## Omniscience

Omniscience means 'all-knowing', from the Latin words *omni*, 'all', and *scientia*, 'knowledge'. To imply that God was not omniscient would be a defect in God, since a defect is a lack of something, and God cannot lack anything. Scholars from as far back as **Origen** in the second century AD have grappled with the problems of God's omniscience. If God knows everything in advance, what is the point of prayer? Equally, if God knows everything in advance are we really free? If God knew how Adam was going to act, is he not partly responsible for sin entering the world?

**Anthony Kenny** (1989) noted that the great Scholastics, such as **Duns Scotus**, **William of Ockham** and **Thomas Aquinas**, failed to agree on how God's omniscience could be reconciled with man's freedom. Ockham held that God cannot know the future, since it depends on the free decisions of creatures. Duns Scotus disagreed and held that God does know the future since he decrees it to happen. Aquinas, with some subtlety, distinguished between something known to happen in the future, and something happening because it was known. He held that if God knows something then *necessarily* it will come to pass, not that it will *necessarily* come to pass! **John Calvin** put forward the difficult view that through his foreknowledge God could predestine people to salvation or damnation and still be righteous. Modern writers tend to solve the problem by suggesting either that God freely withdraws from Himself any knowledge of the future, or by holding – like Ockham – that the future is beyond the horizon of God's knowledge, since it is dependent on the free decisions of creatures. **John Lucas** (1970) holds that omniscience is like omnipotence.

In either case, God can freely choose what He will do or know. **Richard Swinburne** (1977) takes a similar view. In order to preserve His own and humans' freedom, God freely limits His knowledge of the future. In Swinburne's view, knowledge imposes necessity and conflicts with real freedom. God is therefore omniscient in the weaker sense that He wills to limit His foreknowledge. Thus God did not know if Sodom would repent (Gen. 18.22); or if the Pharaoh would let the Israelites go (Exod. 32); or if Nineveh would repent for Jonah – nor did He know the consequences of the angel's warning in Rev. 3.5 that those who repent will have their names written in the book of life. **Keith Ward**, who is influenced by process theology, does not see the future as within God's possible knowledge, since it is not yet a reality.

## Other divine attributes

*God is eternal*
This is often expressed by saying that 'God always was and always will be.' As **Richard Swinburne** put it, God is backwardly and forwardly eternal. 'At no time in the future and at no time in the past can God be conceived as not existing.' The eternity of God is linked to His necessity. In scholastic language, God necessarily exists, rather than contingently, as we do. As **Anselm** put it: 'I cannot conceive of His non-existence.' **Descartes** made a similar point when he said that God's existence was as much part of His nature as the three angles of a triangle are an essential part of the nature of a triangle. **Kant**, of course, objected to this line of argument, pointing out that existence is not a 'predicate'; that is, an applicable quality – such as, for example, when we say that a chair is *comfortable*. The chair by its nature may be comfortable, but we cannot say that God by His nature *exists*. Anselm may well have replied to Kant that the existence of something may not be necessary to understand what it is; for example, dinosaurs don't have to exist for us to understand what they are. But God by His nature is *a special case*. What applies to God does not apply to anything else. As **Aquinas** has put it, God's essence and existence are identical, and God's essence is to exist eternally. More recently, **Norman Malcolm** posed the following conundrum: either God's existence is necessary or it is self-contradictory and therefore impossible. Clearly, it is not self-contradictory, so it must be necessary. For believers, God's eternity forms part of the very notion and mystery of being God, 'the maker of heaven and earth'.

*Eternity and time*
But if God is eternal how is He related to time? This is a major question in theology. Can an eternal, timeless God create a temporal, finite world? **David Hume** argued (naively) that like effects point to like causes; and if the world is finite it is illogical to infer that it must have an infinite maker!

It is clear from the Bible that God acts in time. At a certain time, God created the world of reality. At a certain time, we appeared as self-conscious rational beings on earth. At a certain time, 'God sent his Son' (Gal. 4.4). It would seem to follow from the Bible that God is subject to time, a notion at variance with the classical idea that God is timeless. **Boethius**, in the sixth century, held that God has no temporal extension. 'Thy present is eternity', said **St Augustine**. Neither has God any temporal reference. For God there is no yesterday, today or tomorrow. 'You simply are', said **St Anselm**.

**Aquinas**, facing the question of the relation between God's omniscience and His eternity, asked if God knows things as a succession of events or as a timeless present. Opting for the latter, he believed that God's knowledge cannot be conditioned by time, as is ours. We experience time as a limiting framework: the past is no more and the future is not yet. Surely God cannot be subject to these limitations and restrictions as we are? **Huw Parri Owen** believes that it is unsatisfactory to separate God completely from the temporal nature of the world. God may know events in time 'intuitively', or at a glance, but He knows them as happening successively up to the present. **Richard Swinburne** agrees with Owen and believes that God freely chooses to remain outside time, but allows time to take its course in relation to man's freedom. This means that He lets the future be genuinely free, but subject to His grace and providence. **Jurgen Moltmann** poses the question of how to reconcile the nature of God as eternal and the historical nature of God in the Bible. He says 'an "eternal" God outside time seems too remote to be identical with the God of the Bible'. Process theologians such as **Charles Hartshorne** try to solve this problem with the proposal that God, being 'bipolar', is eternal in His essence, but is subject to time in His dealings with the world (see Chapter 4, Process theology). **Keith Ward** believes that God responds to events in time, but that He is in no way conditioned by time. All that can be said in the end is that questions will continue to remain about this aspect of God's nature. From a philosophical point of view, God cannot be seen to have limitations. But from a biblical point of view, it sometimes appears as if He does.

## God is transcendent

Transcendence is an explicit attribute of God highlighted by many theologians. It is expressed in the Bible in Is. 55.8, and refers to what **Karl Barth** called 'the infinite qualitative difference between the Creator and creatures'. Following the rise of the so-called liberal theology of the nineteenth century, which many traced back to **F. D. E. Schleiermacher** in Germany, there was what Barth saw as an unhealthy stress on the *immanence* of God, an idea which in turn may be traced back to the ancient idea of the *imago Dei*, found in Gen. 1.26. If we are made in

## The Existence and Nature of God

'God's image and likeness', then there are grounds for supposing some continuity between God and man. The resulting trend in liberal theology was to search for those continuities within human nature which might lead to a meeting-point with God, since God is in some way immanent in human nature. This was to forget what **Luther** and the reformers had gone out of their way to stress; namely, the fact that the *imago Dei* in man had been defaced by sin. As a result of this, there could be no way from man to God. The only proper disposition for man to adopt was to recognise his sinfulness, humbly submit himself before the transcendent majesty of God, and thus become a recipient of that grace which alone brings salvation. **Paul Tillich** was concerned to preserve the notion of our dependence on God, and yet felt that it was necessary to get away from the idea that God was some distant figure in the heavens, a notion that people were finding it increasingly difficult to understand. The result was Tillich's proposal to see God as the 'ground of our being', an idea borrowed from the increasingly popular philosophy of existentialism, and which expressed the notion that ultimately we all depend for our fragile, contingent existence on the eternal, necessary existence of God. For Tillich, as for Barth, there was a great chasm between ourselves and God, between the creature and the Creator. In a sense, we partake in a finite way of the being of God. But while we are mere beings, God is 'Being Itself'. Thus did Tillich retain both the *transcendent* character of God, and His immanence as the ground of our being. Another idea highlighted by Paul Tillich was contained in his definition of God as our 'ultimate concern'. As **John Hick** has pointed out, we all have concerns, which may get out of hand or become ultimate. These include such things as pleasure, wealth, status, power, success and so on. However, in due course, as we pursue these they will be seen for what they are: merely earthly and transitory. Only God, who transcends all possible created things, can be the true object of our concern, our 'ultimate concern'. In biblical language, this was expressed in terms of the distinction between worship of the true God and the worship of idols (see Exod. 32.1–10).

The transcendence of God has been affirmed by **Kant**, when he rejected all attempts of human reason to grasp the reality of God. More recently, it has been brought to the fore – ironically – by the arguments of **A. J. Ayer** and the logical positivists. Ayer has argued that because God is transcendent, and not part of the empirical world, all statements about Him are neither true nor false, but *meaningless*.

# Questions about God

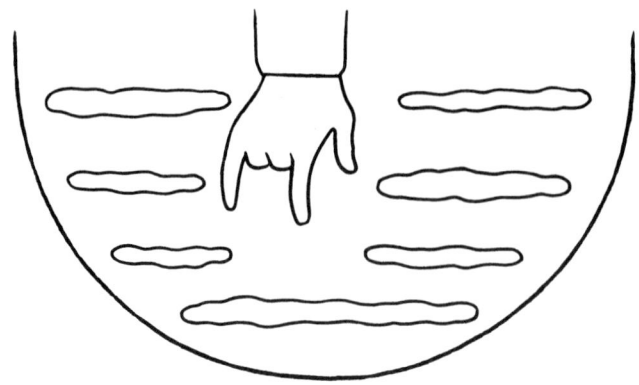

The hand of God in clouds, church of San Vitale, Ravenna, Italy, sixth century. Does this image suggest the transcendence or the immanence of God?

## *God is personal*

**John Hick** has described God as a transcendent 'Thou'. This term was borrowed from **Martin Buber**, who distinguished between persons and things. With things, we form superficial 'I–It' relationships. With persons, we form the much more profound and mysterious 'I–Thou' relationships, of which our relationship with God is the highest form. The nature of God as a person is repeatedly highlighted in the Bible. God's personal nature is presupposed in the very notion of God speaking, commanding, warning, forgiving and so on. In Genesis, God is pictured as working and resting. God is even heard 'walking in the garden in the cool of the day' (Gen. 3.8). To **Moses**, He reveals Himself in personal terms: 'I am who I am' (Exod. 3.14). In the New Testament, Jesus calls God his Father (see, for example, John 14.1–21). Another basis for seeing God as personal is the fact that it is characteristic of persons to love, and 'God loved the world so much that he gave his only Son, so that everyone who believes in him may not be lost but have eternal life' (John 3.16). **Keith Ward** has observed that in the Indian and Greek traditions, God is seen as necessary and immutable. But in the Semitic (biblical) tradition He is seen as personal, creative and active. However, as many theologians have pointed out, we can only apply the characteristic of 'personal' to God not literally, but *analogically*. This means that God is not a *person* in the same way as we are. It means that when we say that God is personal we are applying to God the highest characteristics possible, those we possess ourselves as human beings. **Karl Barth** expressed this another way when he said that God was a *subject*, and cannot be reduced to, or spoken of as if He were an *object*. This takes us back to Martin Buber's point that our relationship to God is an I–Thou relationship, a point supported by the testimony of all the great mystics from **Augustine** to **Teresa of Avila**. **Wolfhart Pannenberg** puts forward the thought-provoking point that we only know ourselves fully as persons after we have experienced God as personal.

Two related attributes follow from the personal nature of God. The first is that God is a *mystery*. A mystery, as **Gabriel Marcel** has pointed out, is something that cannot be fathomed. Persons are, by nature, mysteries. A mystery, like a person, can only be revealed. A *problem*, by contrast, which relates to *things*, can always be solved. God, however, is a unique mystery of infinite proportions, who needs to reveal Himself if we are to know Him at all. The second attribute which follows from the personal nature of God is His *holiness*. This is an attribute profoundly witnessed to by the prophet Isaiah: 'I saw the Lord Yahweh seated on a high throne ... above him stood seraphs ... they cried out ... "holy, holy, holy is Yahweh Sabbaoth. His glory fills the whole earth" ' (Is. 6.1–3).

God's holiness is perceived in His almighty power and majesty. It is this which we recognise in the act of showing reverence, adoration and worship towards God.

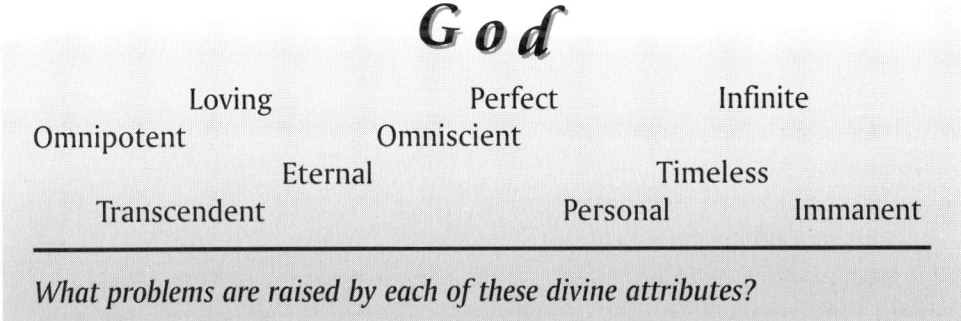

*What problems are raised by each of these divine attributes?*

## II ARGUMENTS FOR GOD'S EXISTENCE

### Anselm: the ontological argument

This is a famous argument, its name deriving from the Greek *ontos*, meaning 'being'. Briefly, the argument (taken from *Proslogion*, Chapter 2) runs like this: God is 'that [being] than which nothing greater can be conceived'. Such an idea exists in the mind, even of those who deny

## Questions about God

God's existence; such as, for instance, the fool in Ps. 14.1, who says in his heart 'there is no God'. Such a person already has some understanding or idea of what he *means in his mind*. However, a being which could only be conceived of in the *mind* would always be inferior to a being which also existed in *reality*. Therefore 'that than which nothing greater can be conceived' must exist in reality. **Anselm** also put it another way (in *Proslogion*, Chapter 3): God cannot be thought of as not existing. That (being) than which nothing greater can be conceived 'exists as truly that it cannot be thought of as non-existent'. Anselm then adds, significantly: 'and thou art this being, O Lord our God'. It is this addition that has led some to believe that Anselm was really doing no more than spelling out what to believers in God is an undisputed truth; namely, that God is an *eternal and necessary Being*. Without these characteristics, or attributes, God couldn't be God. They define His nature as God, in contrast to every other being in existence, which is created and contingent; that is, dependent on something else for its existence. Great as the Big Bang was, for instance, it was only a contingent happening. **John Hick** has expressed agreement with Anselm for showing how the impossibility of God's non-existence makes Him the most adequate object of *worship*. But is there more to Anselm's argument than this? Commentators down the centuries have analysed the argument, and generally found it

## Anselm

*Proslogion*, Chapter 2
God is that than which nothing greater can be conceived ... So he must exist in reality

*Proslogion*, Chapter 3
'I cannot think of you [God] as not existing.'

---

*Anselm originally entitled his Proslogion 'Faith Seeking Understanding'. He also said:*

I am not seeking to understand in order to believe, but I believe in order to understand. For this too I believe: that unless I believe, I shall not understand.

*What is the significance of this for the understanding of his argument?*

at best unconvincing, and at worst invalid. Indeed, Anselm himself had to deal with an objection from a contemporary monk, **Gaunilo**, who mockingly took the example of the *most perfect island*. For it to be the most perfect island, argued Gaunilo, it must be able to exist in reality as well as in the mind! Anselm counters this by insisting that an island, however perfect, could always be thought of as non-existent, 'having a beginning and an end and composed of parts'. But not so God. God, unlike even the most perfect island, is *unique*, and only to God can his argument validly apply.

### René Descartes (1596–1650)

In *Meditations 5*, **Descartes** said that the idea of God was 'in me', the idea of a perfect being to which eternal existence pertains. Anticipating an objection later to be brought by **Kant**, Descartes accepted that it was possible to have an idea of something without it actually existing; for example, I can have an idea of a winged horse even though no winged horse exists in reality – no winged horse that corresponds to my idea of it. Here Descartes seem to be aware of what Kant was to consider the fatal flaw in the ontological argument; namely, that *existence is not part of the concept of something*, or, putting it another way, *existence is not a predicate* – something that adds to the concept, such as colour or size. If this is so, argued Kant, then it becomes impossible to argue from the concept of a thing to the *existence* of that thing. Descartes' reply to this is that the case of God is *unique*. As Anselm before him had said, it is impossible to think of God as non-existent, or in his reply to Gaunilo: 'It is peculiar to God to be unable to be thought of as non-existent.'

## Descartes' triangle

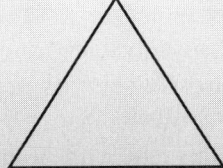

Descartes could no more think of God not existing than he could think of a triangle without the angles being equal to two right angles

*Was Descartes' idea of God logical or existential?*

For Descartes, the idea of a necessary being, for whom existence was a necessary perfection, was a clear and distinct idea. It was not a case, insisted Descartes, of the mind dreaming up the idea of a necessary being such as God is, but the actual reverse. The reality of God as a necessary being *imposes itself* on the mind: 'the necessity of the existence of God determines me to think in this way ... I see clearly that it is necessary that He should have existed from all eternity, and that he must exist eternally' (*Meditations* 5). **Leibniz** would later join those who accused Descartes of arguing from the concept of a thing to its existence in reality, and added sarcastically that because the idea of God's existence was clear to him, it merely begged the question of why it wasn't so clear to others! Leibniz did grant, though – against other opponents – that the idea of God's necessary existence was perfectly coherent. **Aquinas**, it seems, also had difficulty with the logic of Anselm's argument on the grounds that, as a matter of empirical fact, people were not convinced by it. For Aquinas, establishing the *existence* of something was a first step to describing its essence and its attributes.

## Criticisms of the ontological argument

If Anselm's ontological argument is merely a spelling out of his understanding of God *already known to him by religious faith*, then it is largely beyond criticism. There are certainly indications that his argument might be a form of meditation, in which he engages in a theological reflection on the logical, or necessary, attributes of God. This may help to explain his enigmatic prayer: 'Thanks be to thee, good Lord, because I now understand by thy light what I formerly believed by thy gift, so that even if I were to refuse to believe in thy existence, I could not fail to understand its truth' (*Proslogion*, Chapter 4). If this is so, then the argument has clear value to believers, by making explicit what the concept of God means, and leading from this to a worshipful response. **Karl Barth**, a critic of natural theology, saw the great value of the argument in its unfolding for the believer of the implications of religious faith in the biblical God. At the same time, the argument has been interpreted differently, and has provoked lively debate among scholars over many centuries as to its meaning and its validity. **René Descartes** found the argument attractive. He was especially fascinated by the concept of God as a *necessary Being*. For Anselm, necessary existence, the ability to be *self-existent*, was a *perfection* which only God could possess. Descartes agreed with this: 'For it is not within my power to think of God without existence' (that is, of a supremely perfect being devoid of a supreme perfection). Descartes went on to elaborate on this by saying: 'I clearly see that existence can no more be separated from the existence of God than can having its three angles equal to two right angles be separated from the essence of a triangle' (ibid.). At this point, it seems, Descartes went further than Anselm, in explicitly asserting that although a mountain implies a valley, *if a mountain existed*, in the unique case of God it is impossible to say *if he existed*. 'I cannot conceive of God without existence, it follows that existence is inseparable from Him, and hence that He really exists' (*Meditations 5*). **Norman Malcolm**, as we saw, has revived the notion of God's necessary existence by arguing that God's existence is either necessary or it is impossible. Ruling out the idea that it is impossible, he concludes that as an *existential* (rather than logical) fact, God necessarily exists.

## Kant's criticism

A closer look at Kant's criticism of the ontological argument may help to throw Anselm's teaser into greater relief. Kant saw the argument as an exercise in verbal analysis. This means that by analysing the meaning of a word, or concept, it is possible to draw out certain *logical* implications from it. So, for instance, if we analyse the concept *husband* we can see that it logically implies a married male person. It would be therefore *tautological* (circular) to speak of a 'married male husband'. We would not be adding anything *not already contained* in the word 'husband'. Kant distinguished between an analytical statement, which tells us nothing new, and an *existential* or *synthetic* statement, which does. In an existential statement we are saying something about the real world which may be true or false, such as 'it is raining outside'. Such a statement can be *verified* or *falsified*. But, according to Kant, the statement 'God is a necessary being' is *analytical*, not *existential*. In other words, the term 'necessary' is *logically* part of the concept of *God*, but it does not tell us that God exists *in reality*. This means that we can only say, '*if* God exists, His existence is necessary' (similar to 'if a husband exists, he is married). This leads to the second criticism: the idea of something does not imply its existence in reality. Its actual existence is something additional to the idea of a thing. This is what Kant meant when he said that *existence is not a predicate*; that is, it is not a defining quality of a thing, like its size, its shape or its colour. As **Bertrand Russell** explained, unicorns and cows remain concepts in their own right whether or not they actually exist. Russell also made the distinction between a *concept* (for example, a unicorn) and an *instance* of the concept in reality. So, to use Kant's example, the idea of a hundred dollars may correspond to a hundred real dollars, but has no power to make me rich! In the same way, the idea of God does not justify the claim that He exists in reality. We have seen that Anselm's and Descartes' reply would be to appeal to the uniqueness of God. Kant may be correct with regard to everyday contingent things, but his argument is invalid when applied to God. Anselm, Descartes, and more recently Malcolm would insist that the concept God is not a *logical* concept but an *existential* one, and this makes all the difference.

Does the ontological argument work as a proof of God's existence? Perhaps this is not asking the right question. Is it not better to ask: Does it prove God's necessary existence? This indeed it does. But in doing so does it not presuppose that a person already believes in God? Anselm might disagree, if we take into account his claim that everyone has the capacity to understand the concept of God. Descartes appeared to hold the same view. Yet, as Aquinas – ever the realist – pointed out, the existence of God is the very thing which people bring into question. Atheists in particular are not moved by the argument, as the very existence of atheism testifies. **Norman Malcolm** maintains that some sense or experience of human existential need is required to light up the argument, so to speak. An awareness of our mortality and contingency, perhaps, might be a starting point. Malcolm believes that the argument in itself is very unlikely to produce a religious response or lead to theistic conversion. Some sort of religious understanding, it seems, is already required before the argument can be appreciated. In the end, this may well have been Anselm's own view.

## The cosmological argument

The term 'cosmological argument' refers to the procedure of arguing from the *cosmos*, or world, to the existence of God; in contrast to the ontological argument, which makes no use of evidence from the world, but argues by way of analysis from the concept of the greatest, or most perfect, being. The latter is known classically as *a priori* reasoning, while the former is called *a posteriori* reasoning – in other words, after, or based on, the facts about the world. The argument is really in three forms. The first form argues from the fact of *motion*, or *change*. The second argues from the fact of causality, that everything in the world is an *effect* that needs to be explained by a prior *cause*. The third is based on the fact of *contingency*, the fact that everything in the world at one time did not exist, and *might not have existed* except for something else. These three forms of the cosmological argument represent the first three of the famous *Five Ways* of **St Thomas Aquinas**. Before looking at these, it is important to look first at one of the earliest attempts to speculate about the existence of *God* or *the gods*, on the basis of motion and change in the world, that of the ancient Greek philosopher **Plato**, taken from his *Laws*, Chapter 10. Here Plato argues that motion and change, which depend on something prior to bring them about, give rise to the question of how the whole process started. 'How can a thing that is moved by another ever be the beginning of change?' The answer ultimately must be a *self-moving* principle. For Plato, this was *life*, or *soul*. We can see this principle at work in the world in the way living things originate motion and change in other things. But the whole world, said Plato, must be directed by the soul, 'the first moving power and origin of all that is ... the motion which can move itself ... herself a goddess ... a receiver of the divine mind ... a principle of wisdom and virtue which controls heaven and earth and the whole world' so that 'all things are full of gods'. We can see from this line of argument that Plato is not satisfied to accept the world as he finds it. He believes that it requires some explanation, and the explanation which seemed most reasonable to him was in terms of an ultimate self-moving principle superior to anything material, and this is properly called 'life', or 'soul'. **Aquinas** would later identify this self-moving, living principle with the God of the Christian faith.

God creating the world; from a stained glass window, Great Malvern Priory, England, fifteenth century. Plato was the first to put forward a theory of personal creation

## The Five Ways of St Thomas Aquinas

Aquinas, as we have seen, rejected the ontological argument of Anselm with the observation that, had it been convincing, the existence of God would be self-evident to everyone. The fact that people deny God's existence is proof enough, said Aquinas, that it is not self-evident. Believing from faith that God did exist, Aquinas was convinced that there were features of the real world that contained evidence enough to show that God did indeed exist. Putting it another way, if God didn't exist, the world as we know it simply couldn't be explained. The purpose of his *Five Ways* is to show this. Each way (from his *Summa Theologica*) is an exercise of *reason*, not of faith. They are the classic exposition of *natural theology*.

The *first way* is an argument from *motion*. It is evident to our senses that whatever is moved must be moved by something else, and that again by something else. But this cannot go on to infinity, because in that case there would be no first mover. 'Therefore it is necessary to arrive at a first mover, moved by no other; and this everyone understands to be God.'

The *second way* is an argument from the universal fact of *cause and effect*. Everything we experience is an effect, resulting from a prior cause. Nothing in our experience is the cause of itself. To be the efficient cause of itself something would need to be 'prior to itself, which is impossible'. But neither can there be an infinity of efficient causes, because this would rule out the first cause. Without a first cause there would be no subsequent causes. 'Therefore it is necessary to admit a first efficient cause, to which everyone gives the name of God.'

The *third way* follows from the fact that things in nature come into existence and go out of existence. It is possible for them to be or not be. 'But it is impossible for these always to exist, for that which can not-be at some time is not. Therefore if everything can not-be, then at one time there was nothing in existence.' But nothing can come from nothing. We are forced to conclude therefore that there must exist a being which is not merely possible but 'necessary, having of itself its own necessity ... this all men speak of as God'.

The *fourth way* is to be found in the varying degrees of excellence in things. Some things are more, and some less, good, true, noble and the like. This suggests a maximum standard of goodness, truth, nobility and so on. 'Therefore there must be something which is to all beings the cause of their being, goodness, and every other perfection; and this we call God.'

The *fifth way* is based on the fact that everything in the world – both animate and inanimate things – acts towards an 'end' (from the Greek *telos*). This cannot be fortuitous, but happens by design, since things which lack intelligence need to be directed to their end by some being endowed with knowledge and intelligence. 'Therefore some intelligent being exists by whom all natural things art directed to their end; and this being we call God.'

## The Five Ways of Aquinas

| Evidence | Conclusion |
|---|---|
| 1 Motion, change | Prime mover |
| 2 Causality | First cause |
| 3 Potentiality | Necessity |
| 4 Values in things | Highest degree |
| 5 Teleology | Intelligent designer |

*How convincing is Aquinas's masterful reasoning?*

## The cosmological argument: other thinkers

**G. W. F. Leibniz** is credited with having formulated one of the most fundamental of all metaphysical questions, and the one which perhaps underlies more than any other the answer provided by the cosmological argument. The question is: 'Why is there something rather than nothing?' Leibniz went on to formulate a version of the cosmological argument similar to, but also different from, that of Aquinas. In place of Aquinas's observation that every event has a cause, Leibniz observed that every event must have a sufficient reason for its happening. Why there is something rather than nothing also requires a *sufficient reason* to explain why it should be so. Everything in the world requires a reason for its existence, since nothing happens without a reason. But everything in the world can be explained with reference to something else *within the world*. Therefore the ultimate reason why there is something at all rather than nothing must come from outside the world. For a sufficient reason to account for the world of reality, there must be a Being which is able to *create existence*. Such a Being must *necessarily* exist; that is, exist of itself (Latin, *a se*). Because there is something rather than nothing, therefore, a necessary Being exists, which we call God.

*Assessment of the cosmological argument*
There is a compelling logic in the arguments of both Aquinas and Leibniz. They make immediate sense to the believer, and indeed help to expand the believer's horizon to appreciate the ultimacy and indeed omnipotence of God, the 'creator of heaven and earth', as the Apostles' Creed asserts. But they have not proved convincing to the unbeliever. **David Hume** considered the argument an *a priori* one, functioning only to show that the world logically demanded a causal explanation. But this explanation, for all we know, may lie within the nature of the world or the universe. It may be part of the way things are that our universe exists. **Bertrand Russell** was similarly unimpressed with the argument. He declined even to show interest in an explanation or cause for the world, saying that the world was '*a brute fact*', that it was '*just there*'. He cast ridicule on Leibniz's argument, suggesting that you could just as well argue that because everyone in the world had a mother, the human race must also have a mother! It may be that Russell misses the point here. Neither Leibniz nor Aquinas is arguing that because each event in the world requires a causal explanation, the whole series of events that make up the world **also** requires a causal explanation. This would be absurd. Leibniz is simply saying that something in the form of a **sufficient reason**, or **cause**, must bridge the gap between nothing and something. Aquinas is saying that you cannot have an infinite series of things, each of which needs to be explained by something **prior** to it, without demanding how the whole thing started in the first place. **Frederick Copleston**, the great commentator and interpreter of Aquinas, explained to Russell – in their famous BBC debate in the 1950s – that a first cause may be in the order of being (ontological) rather than in the order of time (existential). This means that no matter what happened to explain our world, there must have been some sort of beginning to it all. It may not have been necessary to make this concession to save the argument. There is, after all, scientific support for the emergence of life from a **single cell**, the ultimate 'mother' of the human race!

Notwithstanding the cogency [convincingness] of the cosmological argument, it suffers from the defect of being coldly philosophical and logical. In the end, people are not persuaded by the power of logic. As **John Hick** has pointed out, the argument seems to unbelievers to be begging the question 'Why should the argument stop with God?', or 'Why should God not in turn need to be explained?' Perhaps this very question highlights the big difference between the God of the philosophers and the God of the theologians. To the pure philosopher, God is merely a **concept**, an **idea**.

## The cosmological argument

**Traditional**
Every event has a cause. There must have been a first cause which requires no prior cause. This we call God – Aquinas

**Suggested**
The series of cause and effect raises questions about whether there is an ultimate purpose in the series. To say there is no purpose is to attribute it all to blind chance. To say there is purpose is to invoke a personal or religious explanation

*How valid is the suggested view?*

To the theologian, God is **both** a concept **and** a **reality**. For the theologian there is intellectual satisfaction in being able to demonstrate that what he believes by **faith** can be shown to be a **coherent**, rather than an **absurd**, idea. This is why the cosmological argument continues to have value for believers, despite its incapacity to persuade the non-believer.

## The teleological argument

The teleological argument (from the Greek *telos*, meaning 'end' or 'purpose') became one of the classical arguments of *natural theology*. It is based on the contention that there is evidence of order, purpose and design in the universe and in life. The argument proceeds to conclude that this presupposes a *designer* who is God. The harmonious working of the heavens has struck many as evidence of God's 'handiwork', as

## Questions about God

From the Creation, Bible of Sens, France, c. 1300. What is this illustration trying to convey?

the psalmist put it. The animal world, which runs on instinct, has provided evidence for others to conclude that a hidden intelligent hand orders everything to its appropriate end. Many have been struck by the wonders of faculties such as the human eye. Its perfect design to achieve its purpose, sight, has been used as more evidence of a hidden designer, God.

The argument would lose much of its original force with the arrival of Darwinism in the 1850s, when 'design' was replaced by naturalistic explanations, such as natural selection. It would also be challenged on straight empiricist grounds by **David Hume**, who would argue that appearances can be given any number of naturalistic explanations (see below).

### Paley's watch

One of the greatest exponents of the teleological argument was **William Paley** (1743–1805), in his book *Natural Theology: Or Evidences of the Existence and Attributes of the Deity Collected from the Appearances of Nature* (1802). The best known part of Paley's argument is probably his comparison between the world and a watch. Just as a watch, because it is composed of complex parts ingeniously put together to achieve a purpose, suggests a watchmaker, so does the world, which betrays similar qualities that suggest an intelligent designer.

While Paley's version of the argument is now very dated, the argument itself enjoys something of a revival in terms of the way the world exists at all (see below, and Chapter 2 – for instance, the *anthropic principle*).

---

EVIDENCE OF DESIGN

*In crossing a heath, suppose I pitched my foot against a stone, and were asked how the stone came to be there, I might possibly answer, that, for anything I knew to the contrary, it had lain there for ever; nor would it, perhaps, be very easy to show the absurdity of this answer. But suppose I found a watch upon the ground, and it should be inquired how the watch happened to be in that place. I should hardly think of the answer which I had before given – that, for anything I knew, the watch might always have been there. Yet why should not this answer serve for the watch as well as for the stone? Why is it not as admissible in the second case as in the first? For this reason, and for no other, viz., that, when we come to inspect the watch, we perceive (what we could not discover in the stone) that its several parts are framed and put together for a purpose, e.g. that they are so formed and adjusted to produce motion, and that motion so regulated as to point out the hour of the day; that, if the different parts had been differently shaped from what they are, if a different size from what they are, or placed after any other manner, or in any other order than that in which they are placed, either no motion at all would have been carried on in the machine, or none which would have answered the use that is now served by it.*

William Paley

---

## The Enlightenment critique of natural theology

### Criticisms of Kant (1724–1804)

Immanuel Kant, who credits Hume with 'waking him from his dogmatic slumbers', issued a powerful philosophical attack on the cosmological and teleological arguments. He maintained that all our knowledge was the result of the interplay between what is *observed* and the *observing* mind. When it comes to *causality*, this is something we do not observe. Causality is the result of our minds imposing order on what we see. Likewise, the *apparent evidence* of order and design is again the result of the mind working on what we observe. This being the case, we must confine all our conclusions about order and causality to the world of space and time, the world we live in. *To go outside this world* is to go beyond the range in which the rules of cause and effect apply. Thus, to invoke a *cosmic cause* that transcends the world of space and time (God) is simply invalid. Therefore, the traditional arguments for God's existence collapse.

## Criticisms of Hume (1711–1776)

The Scottish empiricist David Hume was one of the most outspoken critics of the traditional arguments for God's existence. His objections, based on the appearances of things, derived strong impetus from his self-confessed atheism, and probably show how vulnerable the arguments are to an atheistic approach.

Hume first sought to undermine the *cosmological* argument. He attacked the validity of going from the fact of causes *within* the world to some supposed cause *of* the world. Since the world, or universe, could never be *empirically observed* coming into existence, it is invalid to suppose that some cause was required to make them come into existence. To invoke such a cause is to revert to *a priori* reasoning, based on the principle that 'every event must have a cause'. This is a principle that we can accept within the empirical world, but it can have no application *outside this world*. For all we know, the universe may be eternal and not need a cause.

Hume used the same empirical approach to attack the *teleological* argument. This was an argument that was especially vulnerable to such an attack, since it depends on the interpretation of *appearances*. Hume's interpretation would show no sympathy with the religious option. So-called *design*, he argued, could either be the result of the way we *imagine* things to be, or simply the effect of the way things *naturally are*. Here, we may summarise his objections:

1 Even if designed, the universe need not have been designed by a God. The world is finite and full of flaws and defects. If like effects point to like causes, then we have no reason to argue for an infinitely perfect designer, or God. Furthermore, the existence of evil and suf-

fering can hardly support a conclusion of a good, all-perfect God. Maybe the universe was the work of a committee of gods or supermen.

2   For all we know, the universe is unique. There is no evidence that universes, like human artefacts, need designers. They may come into existence naturally, like flowers or vegetables.

3   For all we know, matter may have an inner tendency towards order. A vegetable is the result of order that arises naturally. When we see a vegetable we don't think of who designed it. Likewise, when we look at the universe why think of a clock rather than a vegetable? Vegetables come into existence on their own, naturally. Only artificial constructions such as clocks or watches need intelligent designers. Maybe the universe is like a giant vegetable rather than a giant clock.

4   For all we know, the universe may be the result of pure chance. Maybe particles of matter, falling over infinite periods of time, eventually came together to form our universe.

Hume's objections at least show how easy it is to ridicule some of the traditional arguments of natural theology. However, they remain no more than invitations to view things from an atheistic standpoint, and in this Hume is hardly being original. In the end, Hume's approach is fundamentally scientific inasmuch as he attempts to introduce *natural* explanations to replace supposed supernatural ones. In this respect, Hume was perhaps ahead of his time. Nowadays, the believer is quite prepared to accept from science a more detailed account of how the world is, and indeed how it came about. However, the question which Hume seems to overlook, and the question which the traditional arguments tried to address, is the question of the *ultimate* origin or cause of the universe. Hume's attempt to locate this cause *within* the universe in the end raises the very question that he tries to demolish.

## The moral argument for God's existence

The argument for God's existence based on man's moral awareness is especially associated with **Immanuel Kant**, who famously declared that God's existence could be perceived either 'from the starry heavens above or the moral law within'. Although he undermined the validity of the former, he went on to develop a rather persuasive argument for the idea of

God based on the latter. The link between God and our awareness of right and wrong was already assumed by **St Paul** when he spoke of how the Gentiles, who did not have God's law revealed to them like the Jews, nevertheless had God's law 'written on their hearts' (Rom. 2.15). In his Fourth Way, **Aquinas** argued that our awareness of moral value or excellence (in such things as truth, goodness, beauty, nobility etc.) made us implicitly aware of their ultimate source or cause, God, who possessed these qualities to an infinite degree. Later, **J. H. Newman** (1870) expressed the view that the voice of conscience was the voice of God. Newman argued that our conscience is an implicit pointer to the source of our moral awareness, God. More recently, **Huw Parri Owen** (1971) raised the question of where we may suppose our moral awareness comes from. Either it is a product of impersonal – or chance – existence, or it arises from a personal source that we call God. Owen argues that morality has to do with the personal in life. Using **Buber's** language, it belongs to the realm of 'I–Thou' relationships, not the realm of 'I–It' relationships. Morals and moral values have to do with persons. They make a personal demand on us which is sometimes absolute and inescapable. This points to a source which is not impersonal, but personal – the source we call God. These arguments are not of course persuasive to non-believers. Moral awareness has been shown to be greatly affected by upbringing, cultural conditioning and environment. Others have argued that there is no such thing as an objective moral law. The most that can exist is a set of broad guidelines (such as the Ten Commandments) which need to be applied in the concrete circumstances of life. Thus, for instance, it is wrong to kill, but not in self-defence. If the moral law is not something objective, then it is not possible to speak of a law-giver, such as God.

## Kant's moral argument

Kant believed that it was necessary 'to deny knowledge to make room for faith'. In the moral argument he tried to open up a new approach to the existence of God. He had already shown how God's existence could never be established by the methods of ordinary speculative reason, what Kant called the *theoretical reason*. He now turned to what he called the *practical reason*, a realm of understanding which derives from our practical experience of living in the world. The particular area of experience which Kant would focus on would be our *moral experience*. Our sense of moral duty, or the *categorical imperative*, would enable us to trust, or believe in, the possibility that God exists. Thus did Kant bring about a new approach to the existence of God, an approach that would be taken up by later thinkers such as **Schleiermacher** and **Otto**. It was a change of approach that involved turning away 'from the starry heavens above to the moral law within', as Kant had put it. It would not be a proof of God's existence but merely a postulate, something required for making sense of our human moral experience.

Kant begins by pointing out that we have an inescapable *sense of duty*, what he calls a *categorical imperative* to obey the *moral law*. The moral law for Kant is something objective and real, something we can arrive at by the use of reason. It owes nothing directly to religion. We have an absolute, or categorical imperative (obligation) to obey the moral law if we are to behave as moral creatures. Obeying this moral law means – in Kant's phrase – doing our 'duty for duty's sake'.

Our sense of duty to obey the moral law gives rise to three truths. The first is the *freedom of the will*. If we have a sense of duty this implies that we are able to perform it: 'ought' implies 'can'. By means of his will, man transcends nature. He is not part of nature, as Darwin would imply. This in turn means we must believe in the *immortality of the soul*. Why? Because if not, our sense of the *summum bonum* would make no sense. The *summum bonum* (Latin for 'the highest good') is the ideal or perfect state of affairs when *virtue* will be crowned with *happiness*. This is clearly not achievable in this life. The virtuous are often unrewarded. Obedience and duty to the moral law is often accompanied by frustration and unhappiness. Equally, those who ignore the moral law and shirk their duty often appear more fortunate than the virtuous. This leads to either of two possibilities. Either the *summum bonum* is a figment of the imagination, or it exists in reality in some future realm. If it is purely imaginary, man is doomed to existential frustration: the compelling sense of duty that he experiences ends nowhere. Alternatively, there is someone who is the guarantor of the moral life, someone who in a future realm ensures the equation of virtue and happiness. This calls for the *existence of God*, a more realistic possibility according to Kant, if we are to make sense of our moral experience.

*Assessment of Kant's moral argument*
As we have seen, Kant did not claim that his moral argument was in any sense a proof for God's existence. Historically, the argument has suffered the same fate as the other arguments. It has not been convincing to atheists. But, as **James Richmond** has said, it has proved to have a truly

amazing variability and vitality among believers. The reason for this lies in man's mysterious capacity for transcendence, our ability to go beyond our surroundings and strive after the great spiritual realities of truth and justice. Kant's argument has, therefore, the character of an *invitation* to have faith in the possibility that man's deepest strivings will in the end be satisfied. The alternative is bleak and unattractive: that we are forever doomed to end in nothingness and unfulfilment, after a life lived in transcendence.

Critics of the argument have attacked Kant's claim that there is an objective moral law. Morality, they claim, is the result of convention, and is always changing and developing both between cultures and within cultures. If there is no moral law then there is no *summum bonum*, and Kant's argument collapses. But Kant might reply to this by arguing that because people differ about the *contents* of the moral law, it doesn't follow that such a law is not there. Is it not a fact of experience that we are always striving to know what *is* right and wrong, even after we *think* we know? Even the academic life has a moral character in its relentless search after truth. Truth, like the moral law of Kant, is the object of an endless search, a kind of holy grail, another aspect of man's transcendence, that points to God.

## Updating the arguments

Despite the blow dealt to the philosophical arguments for God's existence by **Hume** and **Kant**, the question of the credibility of theism continues to exercise writers down to our own time. In other words, the enterprise of natural theology goes on. *Kant's moral argument* may be seen as providing a clue to the kind of approach that modern writers have preferred. Kant, having turned away from 'the starry skies above' – the approach that typified traditional natural theology – turned instead to 'the moral law within'. This turning inward in the search for clues to God's existence is now regarded as perhaps the most fruitful way forward in the understanding of God. It takes the form of analysing human experience, and looking for certain gaps and deficiencies that raise existential questions about how they may ever be resolved. Kant's own moral argument was a recognition that there were areas of experience that demanded some kind of explanation, an explanation that must lie outside the horizon of man's earthly existence. Prominent approaches since Kant have included other areas of human experience, such as the emotional, psychological, aesthetic and spiritual. **Schleiermacher** gave up the old rational approach when trying to speak to 'the cultured despisers of religion'. He called attention to the inner 'sense of absolute dependence', which was located deep in the affective nature of the human psyche. We only need a little introspection to sense its presence. James Richmond astutely observed the connection between this approach and Aquinas's concept of contingency, our sense of incompleteness and 'might not have beenness'. **Rudolf Otto** spoke of the capacity to perceive the divine as a haunting presence, a *mysterium tremendum et fascinosum*. This was a presence which was at once attractive and repellent, a mystery which uplifted with joy and paralysed with fear. It is interesting to note that **Sigmund Freud** saw religion as something that penetrated the individual not by rational reasoning but through inner personal, emotional and psychological needs. It was such compelling needs that created the religious *illusion*.

Significantly, Freud's one-time colleague **Karl Gustav Jung** saw religious faith as rooted in *inner personal experience*. Without this inner experience, the outer externals of religious faith, such as dogmas, worship and ritual, he believed, would be rendered empty and meaningless. It is this turning to the inner world of the self, through reflection and introspection, that has become one of the most significant developments in man's recent history in his search for awareness of the divine. **Wolfhart Pannenberg** has argued that man's awareness of his infinite openness to the future which can never be satisfied, and his painful sense of incompleteness as a mortal being, raise the question of God as the ultimate source of his existential fulfilment, a question which is emphatically answered by the Resurrection of Jesus Christ. **John Macquarrie** sees man's existential sense of fallenness and guilt at not being able to reach his true potentiality lighting up the question of God as the Power who can enable man to overcome his weakness and deficiencies. **James Richmond** has argued that our varied human experiences have combined to give us an inescapable sense of the *mystery and contingency* of life. This comes from, among other things, the sense of dissatisfaction with mortal life expresssed by the existentialist writers (including Kierkegaard, Heidegger, Jaspers, Sartre, Camus and others); and, echoing Kant, the 'compelling sense of moral awareness' which we experience, whoever we are or whatever our background. At the same time, there are some modern writers who still appeal to features of the external world to argue for God's existence. **F. R. Tennant** has drawn on aspects of the teleological argument by claiming that a sense of God's presence can be found in the phenomenon of beauty, a striking aspect of the world that simply need not be there. Using a handsome analogy from Acts 3.2, he says 'many enter the temple precincts by the gate Beautiful'.

> **BEAUTY: INTIMATIONS OF ETERNITY**
>
> *It is through aesthetic contemplation that we confront that aspect of the world which was the traditional concern of theology. We cannot prove, by theoretical reasoning, that there is a God: not can we grasp the idea of God, except by the via negativa which forbids us to apply it. Nevertheless, we have intimations of the transcendental. In the sentiment of beauty we feel the purposiveness and intelligibility of everything that surrounds us, while in the sentiment of the sublime we seem to see beyond the world, to something overwhelming and inexpressible in which it is somehow grounded. Neither sentiment can be translated into a reasoned argument – for such an argument would be natural theology, and theology is dead. All we know is that we can know nothing of the transcendental. But that is not what we feel – and it is in our feeling for beauty that the content, and even the truth, of religious doctrine is strangely and untranslatably intimated to us.*
>
> Roger Scruton (1990)

**Austin Farrer** has argued that our sense of *mystery* at the complexity of certain aspects of life raises the question of God. These include not only our sense of moral obligation, but also such things as 'the beauty of landscape and the wonder of sexual reproduction'. All these, he says, are more consistent with a theistic view of the world than any other. **James Richmond** also sees in the external world the basis for a renewed natural theology. These include the empirical world of nature, with all its complexity, the wonder of man's spirit as seen from history, and the testimony to religious faith from believers down the centuries: all these, he believes, converge – to point beyond the empirical to the world of the transcendent.

These writers, in a way, are only attempting to answer the historic question posed by **Leibniz**: 'Why is there something, and not just nothing?'

We conclude this chapter with a look at what is called the 'cumulative case argument'.

## The cumulative case argument

The accumulation of evidence to establish guilt or innocence is a common practice in law, and one with which we are all familiar. In a similar way, we build up judgements about other people perhaps by the unconscious accumulation of evidence based on our acquaintance with them. But can this method be applied to establishing the existence of God? The method involves combining all the known arguments for God's existence to form a composite picture that becomes in the end another argument with its own separate validity. If we arrived in a foreign country to find that all the roads converged to meet at a certain town, we should be justified in thinking that it must be a very interesting place. This analogy can be applied to the various arguments that can, and have been, put forward over the centuries in support of theism. To say the least, belief in theism has proved to be of more than passing interest to countless millions over the years, and many arguments have been advanced to show that it is reasonable.

Other analogies have been less sympathetic to the idea of a cumulative case argument. **Anthony Flew** made the quip that 'If one leaky bucket will not hold water there is no reason to think ten can', to which it can be replied, 'Yes there is, if the buckets are placed inside one another'. Or again, if one piece of wire will not hold a ship to harbour, there is reason to think ten can – if they are twisted to form a cable! The analogy can, of course, be carried further, to discuss whether the cable would break, or how strong it would need to be, and so on.

As in the case of any individual argument, there is no claim that the cumulative case approach is compelling. Theologians are not normally so arrogant as to claim that anyone reasonable enough can be argued into theism. Atheists may claim equal modesty. But what are the main strands of the cumulative argument?

The main strands have already been outlined in this chapter. They include the whole history, and indeed mystery, of revealed theology, from the formation of the Bible to the centuries-old religious traditions that have been built up around it. They include the whole enterprise of natural theology, both in its rational form – running through Paul, Anselm, Aquinas, Descartes and many others to the present day – and its more experiential form, running from Kant, Schleiermacher, Otto and their followers. New strands have been added in modern times. **Wolfhart Pannenberg** has argued strongly for the historicity of the Resurrection. **Rudolf Bultmann** has been in the forefront in making the case for theism on the basis of man's existential experience (see Chapter 4). **Karl Rahner** has written at length on the phenomenon of man's capacity for transcendence as pointing to God for its ultimate fulfilment. **John Polkinghorne** has helped to revive the teleological argument by his treatment of the anthropic principle, the fact of human beings not being explicable on the basis of chance evolution, as proposed by science (see Chapter 2).

Whether this union of different approaches to theism will itself generate a new ground for its credibility will no doubt remain questionable in respect of non-believers, as Flew serves to indicate. But for believers there is bound to be some comfort that so many roads do seem to point to one place – even if, for many of them, none of those roads will be taken.

## Updating natural theology

| | |
|---|---|
| Morality | Kant |
| Dependence | Schleiermacher |
| Numinosity | Otto |
| Beauty | Tennant |
| Mystery | Farrer |
| Contingency | Richmond |
| Fallenness | Macquarrie |
| Transcendence | Rahner |
| Openness | Pannenberg |

*How persuasive are these approaches to natural theology (a) taken individually, or (b) taken together?*

# Chapter 2 | God and Science

## I THE GROWING INFLUENCE OF SCIENCE

According to **Keith Wilkes**, in *The Rise of Modern Science* (1969), the first real signs of true science in the West began to show towards the end of the fourteenth century. This was assisted by the increased use of mathematics, derived from the Arabs. The University of Padua became an important centre for the study of anatomy, mechanics and geometry. The recent invention of printing had made possible the rapid spread of news and ideas. New scientific discoveries were beginning to alter the picture of the world.

## The medieval world view

The medieval picture of the world could be said to have been dominated by three influences: the teachings of the Bible, the philosophical thinking of the Scholastics, of whom **Thomas Aquinas** was the outstanding representative, and the authority of the Church. Aquinas had laid the foundations of a grand synthesis that united all knowledge – rational, scientific and revealed – into a single world view, or overall vision, with God as it's centre. God was the creator and sustainer of the world, which He ruled by the providence of natural law. Natural law was the law of nature: it corresponded to the divine law revealed in the Bible. Both united to reveal a single vision of God's will. The Church's mission was to be the custodian of divine truth, whether rational, scientific or revealed. As **Don Cupitt** pointed out in *The Worlds of Science and Religion* (1976), the whole medieval synthesis was based on the premature assumption that science and faith were in complete harmony. Trouble would come when the empirical aspects of biblical teachings came under question, as they were destined to do with the arrival of the scientific advances of **Copernicus** and **Galileo**. But in the meantime the relationship between science and religion was a happy one. This was illustrated in the way the accepted scientific picture of the universe formed a perfect harmony with that assumed by the Bible.

The picture of the universe and its workings which was accepted by the worlds of both science and religion was the one laid down since ancient times by **Claudius Ptolemy** of Alexandria (AD 100–168). According to the Ptolemaic cosmology, the earth was at the centre, with the sun and the planets revolving around it. This fitted in well with the Bible's teaching that the earth was the special focus of God's creation. It was natural to consider the earth as the centre of the universe, since it was the home of man, the only creature created by God 'in his own image and likeness' (Gen. 1.26), and it was later to be the object of God's redeeming love through the death and the Resurrection of Jesus Christ. Besides, the Bible had clearly assumed that the sun rose and set, as of course it appeared to do: 'The sun stood still in the middle of the sky and delayed its setting for almost a whole day' (Josh. 10.13).

The overthrow of this picture of the universe was to have important implications for the reliability of the Bible's teaching, the authority of the Church, and not least for man's confident sense of his own self-importance. It was to be an early warning of how science could be the bearer of unwelcome news for religion and faith. As events would prove, the Church was to have no choice but to accept the findings of science, however inconvenient they might be. But a more positive and generous approach was already being suggested by scientists. **R. Hooykaas**, in *Religion and the Rise of Modern Science* (1972), describes how **Francis Bacon** (1561–1626) had criticised the intellectualism of the Greeks, and believed that empirical investigation of the world was the best way to honour the Creator. Reluctance to accept the scientific method and the findings that it would uncover would be the makings of an unhappy relationship between religion and science, and would cause much embarrassment for the Church. But science too would play its part in contributing to this unhappy relationship, as we shall see later.

## Copernicus and Galileo

The first great challenge to the medieval world view came from the field of astronomy. **Nicolaus Copernicus** (1473–1543) was a Polish monk who studied at the University of Padua. In his epoch-making book *The Revelation of the Heavenly Spheres* (1543), he cast doubt on the truth of the Ptolemaic cosmology. By using mathematical calculations, he argued that the sun was the centre of the universe, and that the earth, like all of the other planets, revolved around it. His truly revolutionary theory went largely unheeded at first, and was later rejected not only by the Catholic Church but also by the Reformers, including **Martin Luther**. This was an indication of the extent to which such thinking was considered outrageous because of its religious implications. In hindsight, of course, we can see the danger of linking beliefs to *empirical* assumptions which may turn out to be mistaken.

It was not until the scientific work of **Galileo Galilei** (1564–1642) that the calculations of Copernicus were to gain credibility. Galileo was a student at Pisa, but later held the chair of mathematics at Padua. He questioned Aristotle's theories about motion. In a series of scientific experiments, he proved that motion was not something fixed or uniform, but is subject to change. This had important implications in the field of mechanics. Galileo had by now distinguished himself as a practitioner of the scientific method of observation, experimentation, checking and proof. Rationalism and appeal to authority were now being replaced by *empirical observation*. When he used his telescope to observe the heavens, the results could not be ignored. 'It moves!', he was reported as exclaiming, when he observed the earth in relation to the sun.

Galileo was treading on dangerous ground. The Dominican friar **Giordano Bruno** (1547–1600) was condemned as a heretic and burned at the stake for the speculation that there might be other universes. But Galileo knew that he was not indulging in speculation. Here was the testimony of his eyes; here was clear empirical proof. Copernicus was right, but now it can be *seen*: it is indeed the earth that moves, not the sun. The Church authorities were not ready to face the religious implications of this new scientific revelation, so Galileo was silenced. The affair was to create acute discomfort for the Church, and provide a lesson in the futility of challenging science in matters of scientific fact. Galileo is supposed to have said (with great wit and insight), that the Church's job is to tell people *how to get to heaven, not how the heavens go!*

At around the same time, **Johannes Kepler** (1571–1630), a German astronomer, was similarly challenging accepted theories inherited from the past. As a Protestant, he was more free than Galileo to express his private convictions, and had no need to fear Church censure. Yet he too had findings that cast doubt on the established cosmology which was assumed to be perfect and unchanging, reflecting a perfect and unchanging Creator. But it was not only the Catholic authorities that were resistant to change. Luther and the Reformers were equally opposed to the new discoveries because they conflicted with the Bible.

## Questions about God

Why did Galileo provoke such violent criticism from the Church?

A contemporary of both Galileo and Kepler was the Frenchman **René Descartes** (1596–1650). His contribution to the rise of science was through his emphasis on the use of *reason*, rather than authority, as a basis for sure and certain truth. Descartes, in fact, made the first attempt to explain the workings of the universe in terms of *mechanics*. However, his main influence was in the way he separated *mind* (unextending thinking substance) and *matter* (extended substance). Matter was entirely controlled by the laws of mechanics and had its own in-built laws and purposes. Just as mind and matter are separate, so are religion and science. This so-called *Cartesian Split* was to lead to the *Deist* view that God was entirely remote from the world of matter. God was a remote being who once created the world, but left it to run by itself according to the laws of mechanics. With God thus pushed this far out, it was a short step to eliminating Him altogether from the workings of the world.

But the rise of science and scientific method brought losses as well as gains. As Wilkes observed, the medieval world of faith that was now under threat was a world of colour and meaning. The new world of science, concerned with matter and mechanics, was dull by comparison.

## Isaac Newton (1642–1727)

Newton was influenced by Descartes and went on to produce the first really scientific account of the world. Newton was religious by nature, but his science was something that could, to an extent, be kept separate. With Newton, there came a new separation of the heavenly and the earthly, of the natural and the supernatural, of the material and the spitual, of the sacred and the secular. As **Don Cupitt** has remarked, science was now becoming *autonomous*. The scientific method of observation, experimentation, verification and proof was beginning to replace the old reliance on authority and tradition, especially those associated with religious beliefs and the teachings of the Bible.

Newton had spoken of the two books containing all truth, the book of *nature* and the book of the *scriptures*. The former was now the book of science, from which much could be learned; the latter stood for religion and faith. What was significant was the growing use of the methods of science. There was a distinct loss of confidence in the field of religion as a source of truth. The spectacle of religious disputes and conflicts did nothing to restore this loss of confidence. This was coupled with a growing interest in natural or scientific explanations of the way things were. Empirical evidence was becoming widely sought after. **Robert Boyle** had said 'If you want to know about America ask a companion of Columbus'! Philosophical and religious questions about meaning, value and purpose were giving way to more practical down-to-earth *empirical* questions about the way the world was – how it worked and how its secrets could be unlocked. Rational or dogmatic answers were no longer trusted.

## Implications for natural theology

The initial effect of Newtonian physics was to continue the friendly relationship between science and religion. Newton's mechanistic universe, described in *Mathematical Principles of Natural Philosophy* (1687), was for the time being to provide the basis for a convincing *natural theology*. Newton himself saw the way nature worked according to fixed mathematical laws as evidence of the hidden hand of the Creator. 'Where natural causes are at hand', he said, 'God uses them as instruments'. In this way, he found it easy to integrate his scientific findings with his Christian faith, seeing the mechanical order of the universe as a reflection of the perfections of its Maker. As **J. H. Brooke** put it, in *Science and Religion: Some Historical Perspectives* (1991), he was able to see them 'through religious eyes', as indeed was his contemporary **Robert Boyle**.

It was only a matter of time, however, before such confident assumptions would be challenged. **Leibniz** asked how the imperfections of the world could be reconciled with the notion of a perfect Creator. It was still the custom, nevertheless, to use the empirical observations about the world to justify religious faith. **William Paley** pointed to the wonderful order and apparent design in the universe and in the world of nature to argue that it must be the work of an intelligent designer. 'One principle of gravitation causes a stone to fall to earth and the moon to wheel round it. One law of attraction carries all the planets round the sun', he had said.

This was soon to be challenged. Arguing from the facts of the empirical world to some cause – religious or otherwise – that was responsible for the whole and was lying behind the world would be shown to be *philosophically* invalid by **Hume** and **Kant** (see Chapter 1). Now it would also be questioned *scientifically*. The French astronomer **Pierre Laplace**, in his *Exposition du System du Monde* (1813), set out to show that the world could be explained adequately by way of *natural* explanations. He argued that the choice was not between chance and design, but between chance and *mechanism*. The so-called wonder of the planets revolving in the same direction round the sun (which Newton attributed to God's will) was the natural result of atmospheric condensation, the very thing which caused the planets in the first place. When asked by Napoleon about where God was in his scheme, he replied with the now famous words: 'Sire, I have no need for that hypothesis.'

Later, another Frenchman, **Jacques Monod**, would argue that while the universe was a product of predetermined laws and random happenings, it was chance that was the overriding factor (see below).

From these developments, we can see how the so-called 'God of the gaps' became discredited. Filling a natural gap in scientific knowledge with a supernatural explanation, as Newton had innocently done, would now risk being an embarrassing mistake. Science was gaining the competence to provide natural explanations for how things happened in many fields. In the new style of thinking – scientific thinking – there was no room for a religious explanation, and hence the old basis of natural theology was being undermined, if not dismissed. The once happy relationship between religion and science was beginning to break down.

## II THE CHALLENGE OF MODERN SCIENCE

The branches of science that were to create the most serious challenge to religious beliefs were *geology* and *biology*. The challenge from biology would come from the discoveries of **Charles Darwin** (1802–1892), set out in his *The Origin of Species* (1858). But Darwin's findings were built on earlier findings in the field of geology. **Charles Lyell** had argued in *Principles of Geology* (1830) that the earth's rocks were considerably older than was thought. Furthermore, he showed that they must have been formed as a result of *natural* processes over a very long timespan, probably millions of years. Likewise, mountains and valleys must have been formed by natural geological processes, such as uplift, erosion and sedimentation, over a similarly long period of time.

This clearly conflicted with the long-standing belief, based on Genesis, that the earth in its present form was the result of an act of divine creation performed by God over a period of six days (Gen. 1.1–31). Although **St Augustine** had earlier cast doubt on the Genesis timescale, the literal interpretation of the creation story was widely accepted. In the middle of the seventeenth century, **Archbishop Ussher** of Armagh, for instance, had calculated on the basis of the ages of the prophets that creation took place in 4004 BC. The immediate effect of Lyell's findings was to cast doubt on the truth of the Genesis account, and to raise the whole question of the reliability of the Bible.

Today, it is generally accepted that the universe is at least five billion years old, and life on earth to have begun not less than three and a half billion years ago.

Another belief which the Bible seemed to uphold, but which stemmed from **Aristotle**, was that all living creatures had their place in a *Great Chain of Being*, with man occupying a point mid-way between earth and heaven. This came under question when scientists uncovered fossil

## Questions about God

remains that bore evidence of extinct species, millions of years old, that had no conceivable divine purpose, or any place in a 'chain of being'. All these discoveries had begun to undermine the accepted understanding of the Bible, had elevated the credibility of science, and had made the evolutionary theory of Darwin more easy to accept. To this theory we now turn.

Darwin was to have a profound influence on theology. What problems has Darwinism created for the understanding of Genesis?

## The theory of evolution

Darwin was aware of his debt to his predecessors. 'I always feel as if my books came half out of Lyell's brain', he declared. But he was also indebted to the work of **Robert Chambers** and his *Vestiges of the Natural History of Creation* (1843), and Hugh Miller's *Testimony of the Rocks* (1854). Both had done studies on the fossil records, but they had tried to preserve the biblical teaching that the guiding hand of God was behind everything. Significantly, however, both recognised the part that *time* and *nature* played in the development of life. The way was now paved for the acceptance of the idea of evolution.

In 1839, Darwin undertook a long voyage of discovery on *HMS Beagle*, which included a visit to the Galapagos Islands. Darwin noticed that the animals of each island differed somewhat from the animals of another island. He traced these differences to the conditions that prevailed on different islands. Some islands were dry, some wet, some rocky and so on. Those animals that survived on each island seemed to have been the ones that adapted best to their surroundings. Darwin concluded that species *evolved* over long periods of time through this process of adaptation.

This process was called *natural selection*, and was the heart of Darwin's theory in which a natural process was the mechanism of evolutionary change. In the long course of time, only the strongest and fittest were those best able to adapt and survive. This meant that many species failed to adapt, and became extinct. What was to prove troublesome from a religious point of view was that the process was essentially competitive, making it seem brutal, heartless and blind. There seemed to be little sign of any caring, providential hand, one of the key assumptions behind the Bible's message.

For Darwin, this process could account for all the variety of life-forms on earth, so that ultimately all species are variants of a primal ancestor. Darwin, knowing the explosive implications of this for the understanding of the Bible, hesitated for more than 20 years before publishing his findings.

Since Darwin, further findings have given rise to some changes in evolution theory. These now include the role of genetic modifications and other contingencies. In spite of these, the essential view of Darwin has remained practically unaltered. Modern biological evoutionists tend to remain true to Darwin's essentially naturalistic vision. This is reflected in the 1995 official Position Statement of the American National Association of Biology Teachers:

> *The diversity of life on earth is the outcome of evolution: an unsupervised, impersonal, unpredictable and natural process of temporal descent with genetic modification that is affected by natural selection, chance, historical contingencies and changing environments.*

Yet in spite of the apparent bias towards naturalism in this passage, it is not necessarily reductionist. It is still possible to set the process within the framework of a religious vision. This would be, and continues to be, the task facing theologians since the time of Darwin. But their first task would be to cope with the implications of evolution for the understanding of the Bible.

---

Lyell (1830) Chambers (1843) Miller (1854)
↓
They revealed the part played by time and natural causes in the world's development
↓
Darwin – evolution (1858)

*Why did Darwin cause such controversy?*

## Evolution and the Bible

Darwin's theory of evolution was to challenge four important assumptions about life and creation based on the Bible:

1 *Separate creation.* Genesis taught that 'God made every kind of wild beast, every kind of cattle, and every kind of land reptile' (Gen. 1.25). The assumption that God had created every creature separately was taken as an accepted fact. Darwin's theory changed the picture

entirely: through natural processes, everything evolved from a common ancestor.

2 *Instant creation*. The Genesis account described creation as spontaneous and fixed. Darwin's theory undermined this understanding by claiming that all living creatures evolved through a stuggle with their environment over a vast timespan.

3 *Providential creation*. The Bible taught that creation was an expression of the goodness and providential care of God. 'God saw that it was good' (Gen. 1.25). Darwin's theory seemed to cast doubt on this understanding. Evolution seemed, on the contrary, to be driven by natural forces and showed no evidence of any guiding hand. This aspect of evolution shook Darwin's faith. 'There seems to be no more design in the variability of organic beings, and in the action of natural selection, than in the course the wind blows ... disbelief crept over me ...'. It must be mentioned here, however, that a modern writer such as **Thomas Nagel**, although an atheist, raises some very fundamental questions in *The Last Word* (1997) about the capacity of natural selection to explain things such as human consciousness and rationality (see box below).

4 *The uniqueness of man*. Genesis had taught that man was a special creation of God, and was unique among the other animals. Man was made in God's 'image and likeness' (Gen. 1.26). In Darwin's theory, by contrast, man is simply another animal. This was the main argument of Darwin's second book, *The Descent of Man* (1871). Man was now reduced to a product of an evolutionary process that began with a single life-form. In this process, man was continuous with the animals, not different from them. But if Nagel is right (see below), then the last word has not been spoken on this.

---

QUESTIONS ABOUT EVOLUTION

*In spite of the evidence that the entire biological creation, including ourselves, is the product of a stupendously long sequence of chance chemical events, the story is radically incomplete in two ways. First, there is so far nothing but speculation about why the space of physico-chemical possibilities contains this path, and how likely it was, given*

> *the physical state of the early universe, that some path of this very broad kind would be followed. Since it did happen, it must have been possible, but that may be for reasons we do not yet understand. Perhaps the evolution of the universe and of life operates on a much more constrained set of options that our present knowledge of physics would enable us to imagine. Second, the physical story, without more, cannot explain the mental story, including consciousness and reason ...*
>
> *... So my conclusion about an evolutionary explanation of rationality is that it is necessarily incomplete. Even if one believes it, one has to believe in the independent validity of the reasoning that is the result.*
>
> *... I admit that this idea – that the capacity of the universe to generate organisms with minds capable of understanding the universe is itself somehow a fundamental feature of the universe – has a quasi-religious 'ring' to it, something vaguely Spinozistic.*
>
> *... My guess is that this cosmic authority problem is not a rare condition and that it is responsible for much of the scientism and reductionism of our time. One of the tendencies it supports is the ludicrous overuse of evolutionary biology to explain everything about life, including everything about the human mind. Darwin enabled modern secular culture to heave a great collective sigh of relief, by apparently providing a way to eliminate purpose, meaning, and design as fundamental features of the world. Instead they become epiphenomena, generated incidentally by a process that can be entirely explained by the operation of the nonteleological laws of physics on the material of which we and our environments are all composed. There might still be thought to be a religious threat in the existence of the laws of physics themselves, and indeed the existence of anything at all – but it seems to be less alarming to most atheists.*
>
> Thomas Nagel (1997)

Evolution thus appeared to challenge man's cherished status as a child of God, the bearer of God's image and likeness, the *imago Dei* – a status that made him 'little less than a god' (Ps.8.5). Besides, for Christians this gave rise to some uncomfortable implications for the doctrine of the Incarnation and Jesus Christ. In the light of these disturbing implications, it was not surprising that the initial reaction of Church leaders would be to reject the claims of Darwin. As we shall see, not all Church leaders reacted in this way.

# Creation and the Bible

Instant creation
Separate creation
Providential creation
The uniqueness of man

All these assumptions were challenged by Darwin's theory of evolution

*Which caused the biggest problem for Darwin?*

## Reactions to Darwin

As we have seen, the initial impact of Darwinism was to cast doubt on some revered beliefs about the inerrancy and reliability of the scriptures, the role of God as providential Creator, and the nature of man as a child of God. This worried many religious people. Taken at face value, evolution seemed to strip away all supernatural elements in the understanding of life, especially human life, and replace them with natural explanations that required no reference to a creator God. Instinctively, many people concluded that evolution was godless and atheistic. To some extent, this was confirmed by Darwin's later claim that evolution ruled out a divine Creator.

The first outstanding reaction to Darwin came from the Bishop of Oxford, **Samuel Wilberforce**, who took part in a public debate with **T. H. Huxley** (known as 'Darwin's bulldog') in 1860. The Bishop saw Darwin's theory as an affront to the Bible, the dignity of man and the authority of the Church. He spoke on behalf of the values of the traditional biblical view of creation when he said:

> *Man's derived supremacy over the earth; man's power of articulate speech; man's gift of reason; man's free will and responsibility are irreconcilable with the degrading notion of the brute origin of him who was created in the image of God.*

## Questions about God

Ignoring the bishop's taunt about whether he was descended from an ape on his father's or his mother's side, Huxley replied that it was the truth that mattered – nothing else. Unwittingly, Huxley had put his finger on the essence of the dispute between religion and science: the very meaning of *truth*. Confusion between *religious* truth and *scientific* truth has been a major element in the dispute. Whenever one side has invaded the claims of the other on this issue, misunderstandings and a loss of vision have always followed.

It was understandable, but ultimately unwise, for religious leaders such as Wilberforce to invade the territory of biological science, an area of truth about which it was beyond their competence to make any judgement. Equally, it was not on for scientists to make pronouncements about – and, much less, reject – religious claims which did not contradict, and could possibly be consistent with, their scientific findings. As a contemporary scientist, **Hoimar von Diffurth** (quoted by J. Morin, in *How to Understand God,* 1968), put it:

> *If, from the indubitable fact that the world exists, someone wants to infer a cause of this existence, his inference does not contradict our scientific knowledge at any point. No scientist has at his disposal even a single argument or any kind of fact with which he could oppose such an assumption ...*

## Views of man

**Scientific**
Man is a life-form produced by evolution and sharing a common ancestor with the other animals

**Religious**
Man is a special member of creation, made by God in his image and likeness and redeemed by Jesus Christ

*Can these views be reconciled? How can the scientific view become 'reductionist'?*

## Positive responses to evolution

One of the earliest Church leaders to give a favourable response to Darwin's findings was the Archbishop of Canterbury, **Frederick Temple**. Temple saw no conflict in principle between evolution and the teachings of the Bible. Genesis was a *religious* text concerned to teach a religious message. It was not a *scientific* document. This enabled Temple, in the Bampton Lectures of 1884, to welcome Darwinism in principle, while at the same time defend the spiritual validity of the Bible's message. As he put it: 'In conclusion, we cannot find that science, in teaching evolution, has yet asserted anything that is inconsistent with revelation ... There is nothing in all that science has yet taught that conflicts with the doctrine that we are made in the Divine Image.'

Another leader to show a positive response to Darwin was the vicar and author **Charles Kingsley**. For Kingsley, evolution did not detract from but enhanced the glory of God: 'We used to say that God was so wise that He could make all things. Now we know that He is much wiser than that. He can make all things make themselves.'

In those words, Kingsley was showing an optimism that many believed was undermined by the scientific evidence. Evolution appeared to be a random process, driven by sometimes ruthless natural forces, with seemingly no guiding hand behind it. As **Don Cupitt** has put it, 'Evolution revealed a world more haphazard than rationally ordered, a world without apparent purpose.'

It would be the task of subsequent theologians to set evolution within a *theological* framework, and show how it could be reconciled with belief in a loving God. Nobody took on this task with greater vigour than the French palaeontologist and priest, **Pierre Teilhard de Chardin** (1881–1955). For him, evolution was a divinely willed process with its own in-built dynamic. It was a process which led in an ascending line from inanimate matter to the arrival of life, from primitive life to the arrival of man himself, the high point of whose development was the person of Jesus Christ.

Thus did evolution embrace the biological, the human, and the moral or spiritual. With this vision, Teilhard de Chardin anticipated the *anthropic principle*, the notion that the universe was intended to produce conscious life. His vision was regarded as too speculative by scientists, and too optimistic by his Church. Whatever its credibility, it was an imaginative attempt to embrace the new science, and reconcile it with religious faith (see box).

> PIERRE TEILHARD DE CHARDIN
>
> As a priest and scientist, Teilhard de Chardin was in a unique position to bridge the divide between religion and science. He saw science as a potential source of divine truth. 'All roads of truth lead to the One God', he said. There were four key concepts in his thought:
>
> 1 *The law of complexity*. This meant that matter had within itself the tendency to evolve into more complex states. Teilhard called this the 'psychic' aspect, present in matter from the very beginning. This in-built drive towards ever more degrees of complexity led eventually to the emergence of *life*, and eventually *human* life.
>
> 2 *Radial energy*. This is a dynamic force inherent in physical structures, which eventually manifests itself as *love*.
>
> 3 *The Spirit of God*. Everything is under the influence of the Holy Spirit, who dwells within creation, and is the source of its dynamism. Under the influence of the Spirit, radial energy causes increasing complexity, which leads ultimately to human personality, the high point of which is human love. The Spirit charts a path which begins at an *alpha point* (primal matter), and ends at an *omega point* (human salvation).
>
> 4 *The Incarnation of Christ*. This enables man to reach the omega point, of which Christ himself is the human manifestation. Because of its final destiny of 'Christification', all matter is sacred.
>
> *The spheres*
> In Teilhard's thought, reality is divided into spheres of existence:
> - atmosphere – the sphere of gas enveloping the earth
> - lithosphere – the crust enveloping the earth
> - hydrosphere – the sphere of water, necessary for life
> - biosphere – the sphere of living things
> - noosphere – the sphere of conscious communication (human life)
> - Christosphere – the sphere of brotherly love between human beings

## The challenge of cosmology

If biology was the source of the main challenge to the Bible and religious faith in the nineteenth century, it was cosmology which added to the challenge in the twentieth. For **Keith Wilkes**, the main issues raised for theologians by twentieth-century cosmology were ones already raised by Darwin; namely, the relationship between God and creation, and the place of man within the universe at large.

The hand of God superimposed on a pagan sun-disc, from the Cross of Muirdeach, Monasterboice, Ireland, seventh century. What idea does the picture convey?

Two main theories of the origin of the universe have been put forward. The 'Big Bang' theory was first put forward by **Georges Laimatre** of Louvain in 1927, and further developed by **Edwin Hubble**. A rival theory, called the 'Steady State' theory was put forward by **Fred Hoyle** in The Nature of the Universe (1948). In this theory, matter and energy are constant throughout the universe, which had no apparent beginning. 'I find myself forced to assume that the nature of the universe requires continuous creation – the perpetual bringing into being of new background material.'

In this view, the amount of matter in the universe remains the same, within a constant framework of decay and renewal. In the Big Bang theory, a cosmic explosion of dense matter some 13 billion years ago created time and space. As the earth cooled down, chemical reactions took place that eventually led to the emergence of primitive life-forms, from which all life, including human life, evolved. This view has been challenged very recently by **Sir John Maddox** in What Remains to be Discovered (1998). He says:

## Questions about God

> *The Big Bang is a good fairy tale. You can tell it to the children, and they understand it. But it doesn't give a coherent account of how galaxies form; and new things are happening which add yet further doubt. Nothing in the Big Bang theory explains why the early universe should behave in the way it now appears to be behaving. The universe does not seem to be as uniform as everyone assumes. And if it isn't, then all the calculations to do with relativity are going to have to be redone in much more complicated ways.*

Whichever view is accepted, we know from carbon dating that the universe is extremely old (the carbon clock, discovered by **Libby** in 1949, made it possible to date with considerable accuracy the age of rocks and fossils). This puts it in conflict with the Genesis account, if the latter is taken literally.

Cosmology has also altered the *religious* perspective of the world, traditionally seen as the special object of God's love. Far from being the centre of the universe, earth is now seen as a small planet in a minor solar system, which may be one of a thousand million galaxies. In this scenario, the traditional belief that man is unique, and the special object of God's love, becomes more difficult to comprehend. So also is the traditional belief that God created the universe in the way described by Genesis. Once again, the task for theologians was to find an accommodation between the compelling discoveries of science and the basics of Christian belief.

For the Swiss theologian **Hans Kung** (1980), the main question arising from the new cosmology was *existential*. It was the question of whether or not life had meaning. Did the world come about by *accident* or by *design*? If by accident, then it becomes an almost impossible task to give an overall meaning to life, one of the great contributions of religion. Could the Big Bang be seen within the framework of a divine plan?

Scientists such as **Jacques Monod** have argued that everything is the product of blind chance. In his book *Chance and Necessity* (1972), Monod argues that natural processes follow a predetermined path (necessity), in conjunction with unexpected happenings that may be attributed to chance. He states, 'Pure chance, absolutely free but blind, is the very root of the stupendous edifice of evolution.' Here, it could be argued, Monod is going beyond the strict confines of science, to postulate a *metaphysical* theory as a rival to a religious one. Since a theory of chance could never be proved right or wrong, it raises questions as to whether it could qualify as a strictly *scientific* theory.

## Interpretation of scripture

| Fundamentalist | Conservative | Liberal |
|---|---|---|
| The Bible is the Word of God and must be accepted literally. Its contents are a challenge to faith, but they cannot be underminded by science | The Bible should be taken literally unless there is a good reason not to. The Bible is essentially a spiritual book and may have some material errors. The Bible is a divinely inspired book containing God's revelation | The Bible is a human production that needs to be understood in the light of its time. To understand its spiritual message, it may be necessary to discard some of its empirical descriptions. But its essential message is beyond the province of science |

*What are the similarities and differences between these views?*

## The science of history

Alongside the challenge to biblical authority raised by the sciences of geology and biology, which we have just seen, came another challenge of a more direct kind. As **J. H. Brooke** (1991) put it, 'The most radical challenge to biblical authority came not from the history of science, but from the science of history.'

The new science of history was to call attention to the famous dictum of **G. E. Lessing** (1729–1781), who was sceptical about discovering the truths of history: 'The accidental truths of history can never become the

A dove in the waters of creation; a reproduction of a thirteenth-century image, taken from Auxerre Cathedral, France. Teilhard de Chardin saw the Spirit of God as permeating the whole of creation

proof of the necessary truths of reason.' Lessing's words were now applied to the Bible as an historical book. Maybe the truths of faith, like the truths of reason, should be independent of the accidental truths of history. Anyway, what were those truths of history? Like other documents of history, the Bible became subjected to what came to be called the *historical–critical method*. This involved setting a document within the context of its time in order to examine the human and cultural influences that shaped its contents.

An area of special focus was the gospel accounts of the life of Jesus. In his study of the gospels, **D. F. Strauss** (1835) claimed that the miracle stories, and other supernatural elements in the life of Jesus, could be understood as well-intentioned insertions by the early believers, but had no basis in fact. They were woven back into the story of Jesus because such miraculous events were expected in the time of the Messiah. 'The resurrection was a delusion, but not a fabrication', he declared.

Strauss was dismissed from his post for his anti-religious ideas, but the historical–critical method of investigating the Bible is now an accepted fact. The Genesis story of creation, for instance, is now seen as part of a wider context of creation stories which were current at that particular time. Thus did the science of history bring to light how human factors played a crucial role in the religious ideas revealed in the Bible.

It also raised, in particular, the important question about in what sense the Bible can be said to be the 'Word of God' if it is written by human beings in human words. The traditional understanding of the Bible was that its writers were 'divinely inspired' when writing its contents. This was now seen to be an oversimplification. If they were inspired, their inspiration could not be understood without some reference to the influences and conditions that prevailed in their time.

It is now beyond dispute that the new historical–critical method made it possible to understand the so-called scientific 'errors' in the Bible. As a product of pre-scientific times, it was natural that its writers would have been unaware of scientific facts about the world which only became available centuries after they wrote. This insight made it possible for theologians to separate the religious message of the Bible from the outmoded science in which it was often framed. Strauss, for all his indiscretion, had set biblical criticism on the right lines. But he had not shown that the truths of faith could be completely separated from the events of history. This would continue to be a contentious area of debate among theologians to the present day.

## Negative responses to modern science

### Fundamentalism

Aggressive marketing of evolutionary and other modern scientific ideas had the effect, for many people, of making them believe that science was atheistic and godless, and indeed that the aim of scientists was the elimination of God from an understanding of life and the world. This conviction led to the formation of so-called 'fundamentalism' in America, and its offspring, 'creationism' (see below).

The term 'fundamentalism' is derived from the five 'fundamentals' drawn up by the Presbyterian General Assembly in 1910. They included the acceptance of the literal truth of the Bible, the divine status of Jesus Christ and his atoning death for sin on the Cross, his bodily Resurrection, and the reality of heaven, hell and the devil. Evolution was a particular target of the fundamentalists. The idea that the world could be explained by natural causes threatened the whole belief system of the Bible, including the very status of the Bible itself. Once a single belief is undermined, it was held, all other beliefs collapse like a house of cards. No creation means no redemption, no need for Jesus Christ, no Resurrection and no after-life. Fundamentalist attitudes to evolution were famously revealed in the Scopes Trial of 1925, when a teacher from Arkansas was prevented from teaching evolution to children because of the dangers it would cause to faith.

# Fundamentalism

The Bible is the 'Word of God'. There can be no separation of its spiritual truth from its material truth. Some parts of the Bible are a test of faith. What science says is essentially godless and misleading if the Bible says otherwise. The first three chapters of Genesis are crucial for understanding the story of Redemption

*Do fundamentalists pay too high a price for holding on to their beliefs?*

## Scientific creationism

Creationism in the widest sense is the belief that, ultimately, all reality is the product of the creative will of God. All believers, therefore, are creationists of some kind, stretching from ultra-conservative to ultra-liberal. Creationists of the fundamentalist kind, sometimes called 'young earth' creationists, represent the ultra-conservative position. They believe that creation took place literally in the way described in Genesis.

They received a setback in 1968 when a US Supreme Court ruling declared their beliefs unconstitutional, because they were essentially *theistic*, and therefore religious. They then attempted, through their spokesman **Henry Morris**, to establish creationism as a scientific theory that deserved to be taught as a secular 'scientific' rival to evolution. They called it *scientific creationism*. Their application was rejected on the grounds that it failed to qualify as a scientific theory. Any theory that is not prepared to be altered or confirmed by later scientific discoveries is not strictly *scientific*. This was later upheld by the US Academy of Sciences (1972), which declared 'science and religion to be mutually exclusive realms of human thought' for this reason.

According to Morris, there are four dogmas of scientific creationism:

1 the special creation of all things in six days

2 the curse upon all things by the Fall, resulting in the gradual deterioration of the entire cosmos

3 the universal flood, which drastically changed the rates of most earth processes

4 the dispersion of Babel, which accounts for the proliferation of languages and cultures

*The gap theory*
This was an attempt to bridge the age gap between Genesis and the geological findings that the earth was millions, not thousands, of years old. It was first proposed by **Thomas Chalmers** in 1814. He argued that the gap can be explained in terms of the first two verses of the creation story in Genesis Chapter 1. Verse 1 says, 'In the beginning God created the heavens and the earth.' Verse 2 says, 'Now the earth was a formless void, there was darkness over the deep.' After the original creation, it was argued, there occurred the Fall of Satan and the wicked angels, which resulted in the collapse of the world into chaos. Only much later did God create the world as we know it – in six days, including the special creation of man.

The creationist **A. J. Monty White** rejects this theory as unnecessary to preserve a literal reading of Genesis (see below).

Creationists also have serious difficulties in reconciling a literal reading of the Bible with the findings of biological science. From the fossil records, for instance, it can be seen that they follow an orderly pattern: older fossils are found in older rocks, and younger fossils in younger rocks. If the Genesis flood had caused the fossils, they would all have been of the same age, and distributed in a totally random fashion in a single rock layer. Besides, the sheer volume of fossils (800 million alone in the Karroo formation in Africa), defies the flood theory in the same way that modern science shows the earth to be millions, not thousands, of years of years old.

Creationists have responded to these claims with the reply that God, by miraculous means, has altered the fossil record as a test of faith. This has led to the distinction between the *actual* age of the earth, and the *apparent* age of the earth. In this view, the earth was created according to Genesis about 10 000 years ago, but has an apparent age of millions of years.

This view has been expressed by **A. J. Monty White** in *How Old is the Earth?* (1985): 'We can see clearly that the Bible teaches that God created a mature creation that had a superficial appearance of age.' He dismisses the theory of evolution as a prejudice that forces a reading of rocks and fossils as millions, not thousands, of years old! The refusal of creationists to yield to scientific advances that conflict with the Bible is a reflection of their concern to preserve the religious and moral implications of the Bible's message. But many would argue that this is too high a price to pay for something that can be preserved and upheld in harmony with evolution.

## Views of the world

| Scientific | Religious |
|---|---|
| The world is a natural product of a scientific event that took place 20 billion years ago. It was probably a random, or chance, event | The world was ultimately intended to exist by God and is sustained by his power. It is the testing ground for man to work out his salvation |

*At what point does the scientific view as stated involve agnosticism or atheism?*

## III SCIENCE AND RELIGION: CAN THEY BE RECONCILED?

### Some preliminary issues: different causalities

Modern scientists such as **Richard Dawkins** adopt an atheistic attitude to the world on the grounds that the available evidence cannot support belief in God. This is not an unreasonable stand (one, in fact, that Kierkegaard would agree with). However, it should lead to *agnosticism*, as opposed to atheism, and leave aside the idea of God as an option that must be either accepted or rejected. An atheistic view that rejects belief in God as an *ultimate* explanation of reality and replaces it with *chance* (as Monod did) is just as much a metaphysical view as the one it opposes, the religious view.

## God and Science

The historical tendency of religious leaders to assume that natural explanations were a rival to supernatural explanations (and, as a consequence, to oppose scientific advances in knowledge) has, no doubt, led scientists to use their science as a stick with which to beat religion. The problem has been that many of the conflicts between religion and science have had their origins in mistaken understandings of causality. Dawkins appears to think that religion is in competition with science in providing *causal explanations* of events. Unfortunately, fundamentalist attitudes to science have provided ammunition for this kind of view. **C. Stephen Evans**, in *Philosophy of Religion* (1982), has made the important point that mainstream Christian thinking does not see religion as a rival to science in providing explanations for natural happenings, or in influencing the way things happen. This mistaken view of causality was held by **Comte** when he said that religion would be replaced by 'more enlightened' science. But as Evans points out, it was *mythology* and *magic* which have been replaced by science, not religion.

This kind of mistake is still being made by scientists such as Dawkins. He indiscriminately treats fundamentalist ideas as examples of modern religious attitudes to science, and regards shops that deal with magic and the occult as more examples of 'religion'. Dawkins shows no awareness of the tradition of self-criticism in the history of the Church, part of which was sorting out faith from superstition, magic, the occult and other aberrations.

More enlightened thinking today (thanks in part to science) recognises that religion is about *theological*, not *causal*, explanations. A theological explanation can be consistent with whatever scientific explanation is established as correct (for example, how the universe came about, or how life began). Theology simply says that there is something *more ultimate* than all natural explanations (see also below). **Keith Ward**, in *Holding Fast to God* (1982), makes the same point:

> *It is precisely science, which seeks the greatest possible rational explanation for things, which leads to the conjecture of a final explanation for everything. That ultimate conjecture is bound to be beyond the scope of any particular science ... The success of the sciences is the best argument for theism there is, for it leads us to seek ever-more complete explanations for things.*

## Explanations

**Causal**
Science provides causal explanations in teams of natural or scientific laws. No other explanation can be visible to scientific investigation

**Theological**
Theology offers ultimate explanations in terms of personal agency acting through scientific laws. An exception may be made (in principle) for miracles

*Is this a valid distinction?*

As we shall see in the next section, this understanding will form the basis of a new reconciliation between science and religion, as proposed by some modern theologians.

## The responses of modern theologians

In this section, we look at the thought of four British theologians (Adam Ford, Arthur Peacocke, Russell Stannard and John Polkinghorne), all of whom may be called 'theologians of science'. All may be considered representative of recent attempts to reconcile Christian theology with the findings of modern science. All agree that science and theology must form a partnership in man's search for a total meaning to life. All agree that science can throw important light on how the world works, and therefore on how God works. All agree that there is room for a metaphysical understanding of life, and this science is unable to provide. All agree that science on its own can only provide a partial account of why the world is as it is. All agree that religion, while taking the truths revealed by science into account, helps to complete the picture, and provide a wider perspective on reality in the light of man's emotional, historical, ethical and spiritual nature. All these, it can be claimed, are aspects of the human condition which lie outside the vision and the grasp of science.

### *Adam Ford*
In *Universe: God, Man and Science* (1986), Ford expresses his belief that science and faith can coexist in harmony with each other. Here is a summary of the leading ideas from his book:

- The possibility of evolution was mentioned by St Augustine as early as the fourth century. Evolution is not inconsistent with belief in God as ultimate Creator.

- Evolution changes the picture from the finished product (the Garden of Eden) to a slowly developing ecosystem, that involves mutations, failures and random extinctions over immense periods of time.

- This changes the picture of God from Creator 'in the beginning' to an active living Spirit, operating within the whole process. This process includes chance as well as law.

- Evolution appears to be both natural and without direction or purpose. This helps to create a non-theistic view of the world. God appears an unlikely hypothesis.

- If Genesis is viewed as myth, and not as science, important benefits will result for a fuller understanding of the world. In particular, the world and human life will not be seen as products of blind chance.

- Evolution, however, does away with the old idea of a designer God, as classically represented by William Paley. A new understanding of God is therefore required by the facts of evolutionary biology.

- The big problem raised by evolution is how such a chance or random process can leave any room for a traditional Creator.

- The answer lies in the way in which law and chance can be combined. From a biological point of view, chance is the outstanding feature. From a theological point of view, chance is part of a purposeful process.

- The ultimate purpose behind the process of evolution was the development or emergence of human life. God played dice (chance), but He had already laid down the rules.

- The appeal of fundamentalism and the literal interpretation of scripture lies in its concern to preserve the place of God, as well as the dignity and purpose of human life. But these aims can be achieved without sacrificing the findings of modern science.

- Man's highest faculty is his reason. The highest glory God can receive is through the responsible use of reason. The pursuit of scientific truth is one such use.

- Science and faith should be in perfect harmony. Nobody tried to achieve this more than the French theologian of evolution, Pierre Teilhard de Chardin. The evolutionary journey from primitive matter through human consciousness to the life of Jesus Christ is a process that is infused with the Spirit of God. The final stage of evolution is man's journey on earth towards God.

### Arthur Peacocke

Peacocke's thought is contained in *Cosmos, Man and Creation* (1979), *Creation and the World of Science* (1979) and *God and the New Biology* (1986). Here is a summary of his leading ideas:

- Evolutionary ideas were widely seen as a threat to religious beliefs, by appearing to undermine (a) the truth of scripture and (b) traditional ideas about the divine origin of man.

- In the light of Darwin's theory, it was now going to be more difficult to hold on to the belief that man and his so-called higher faculties had any special significance over and above the animals.

- Theology cannot run away from the truths of science. A constructive response to Darwin was required to make the Christian faith consistent with what is true about the nature of the world as revealed by science.

- The Huxley–Wilberforce debate produced more arrogance among theologians than was warranted by the findings of Darwin. The result was an uneasy truce between the reconcilers and the irreconcilers.

- In the twentieth century, Karl Barth has called for a 'retreat to the citadel', and refused to welcome any contribution from the world of science, because he felt that the Christian faith should never be put at the mercy of scientists. More recently, a thaw has set in with the realisation that truth is one, no matter from which side it comes.

- A change of attitude is needed from both sides. Scientists need to recognise a metaphysical need for more awareness of the *ethical* dimension of the practice of science. Theologians need to recognise the need for a more humanistic approach to understanding the way God works. God's action is as much present in the world of science as in the pages of the Bible. Even the Bible itself must submit to the criticisms of science.

- The fundamental truth of Genesis 1 and John 1 is that everything depends on God's will. Yahweh is He who causes to be. God's action in the world is not limited to the very beginning (Deism). It also embraces the course of history (Moltmann, Teilhard de Chardin). This view is the real view, not imposed from above by authority, but derived from the experience of God in human life.

- This view cannot be compromised even if it is only disclosed by faith.

- This means that the world is not the result of blind chance as Monod had held. But how the world operates is the true province of science. The more science discloses about the world, the more it discloses about God. Thus, from a theological point of view, religion must be respectful towards science. Equally, science must allow religion the validity of its perspective.

- Acording to leading German theologian Wolfhart Pannenberg, theology has an important part to play in providing an avenue to the *total* truth about reality. This is not possible for science.

- Science and reality are two interacting approaches to the exploration of the nature or reality.

- As regards the nature of man, science only sees a continuity of nature and development from the lower animals. Theology calls attention to the fact that man differs from the lower animals by his ability to transcend his environment and shape his destiny.

- Theology also has the means to give an account of man's nature as essentially injured or 'fallen'. This is described in the Genesis myth of the 'Fall', and is about man's present state of alienation from God.

- The analytical nature of science, its tendency to divide things into parts, makes it ill-suited to satisfy man's search for an all-embracing and comprehensive understanding of reality as a unified whole. Science itself is now beginning to appreciate how all things are interconnected – as, for example, in regard to ecology.

- The activity of God cannot be separated from the natural processes of cause and effect seen throughout the whole of creation. God is immanent in creation and in the working of its laws, yet remains transcendent.

## Russell Stannard

Stannard's views are contained in his *Grounds for Reasonable Belief* (1989). Here are some of his leading ideas:

- Invoking the explanation 'God' is no more than trying to solve a problem by giving it a name.

- Science has to confine itself to physical explanations.

- Our universe might be the kind that expands and contracts for ever.

- Evolution dispenses with a designer God. Natural selection is a perfectly adequate explanation for what looks like good design.

- But actually the design argument has made a surprising comeback in recent years. While life appears to evolve at random, the conditions required for life to exist at all cannot be taken for granted. Even the Big Bang had to be precisely right for life to emerge at a later date. Furthermore, great precision was required for the formation of carbon, the essential raw material of all living things.

- Scientists, of course, might reply to this by arguing that ours may be the only one of millions of universes actually to produce life.

- All attempts to find a place for the operation of God in the physical world – either through normal events seen as signs of God's activity (such as thunder and lightning), or through unexpected events seen as miracles, have been ruled out as unscientific, or without foundation.

- Therefore, any discussion based on scientific assumptions about what constitutes total reality is seen to rule out the whole idea of God.

- Theology and science have much in common: they are both engaged in the search for truth. At the same time, they are different in that each has a different kind of object. For science, it is an impersonal *it*; for religion, it is a personal *thou*. Science involves the pursuit of the brain and the intellect. Religion takes into account the whole person, which includes not only the act of understanding, but also the search for an all-embracing appreciation.

## *Scientific advances*

| Cosmology | Geology | Biology |
|---|---|---|
| Earth not centre of universe. Everything began from a Big Bang explosion billions of years ago, or has existed for unknown time – at variance with Genesis if taken literally | Rocks and fossils show the earth to be billions of years old. Geological evidence shows pattern of natural causes. No evidence to support biblical flood or instant creation | All life began with single cell, resulting in evolution from common ancestor. Natural selection explains process of evolution of different species. Serious implications for literal reading of Genesis |

*How have theologians responded to these advances?*

*John Polkinghorne*
The following summary of Polkinghorne's ideas is taken from his *Science and Creation* (1988) and *Reason and Reality* (1991):

- Theology is concerned with finding the deepest possible level of understanding of the world. The religious view of the world is the *total* view of the world.

- Theology must take into account all other forms of knowledge and truth. This includes scientific knowledge. Theology just cannot be left to theologians.

- Natural theology is the search for knowledge of God by the exercise of reason and the inspection of the world. This is an important endeavour today when so many reject theism as incredible.

- The complexity of matter is something that modern physics is only beginning to appreciate. This very complexity has parallels in the field of theology. Theology is often accused of not speaking clearly of its subject. But science is now having to face the same accusation.

- Old-style natural theology, based on ideas of order and perfection, must be replaced with truths and ideas from modern science. Yet Aquinas's idea that God is logically the first and originating cause of everything still holds validity.

- As Wolfhart Pannenberg has said, history as well as science can provide vital knowledge of God and His will. Revelation must not be put in contrast with natural knowledge. Science can also be a source of revelation.

- The very intelligibility of the world which makes it open to scientific inquiry raises deep questions that science is unable to penetrate.

- Science and theology are intellectual cousins under the skin. They are both engaged in rational inquiry into whatever we experience. For theology, the nature of its object (God) determines what can be known. God cannot be produced for inspection. God is a *subject* (a thou), not an object (an it). As Pannenberg put it, theology is the study of reality from the point of view of God.

- The pursuit of theology is truth. But truth can be seen in terms of 'correspondence' or 'coherence'. The former is concerned with accuracy of fact, and is the province of science. The latter is concerned with what 'makes sense' to an understanding of life, and is the concern of theology.

# The teleological argument

**Old form**
The universe and nature, including man, show evidence of order and purpose analogous to the way a watch is designed to tell the time – Paley

**New form**
Nature might have within itself a tendency towards order (Hume), but the sheer fact of an intelligible world observable by man raises questions to which theism provides a credible answer – Polkinghorne

*How can the two arguments be compared?*

## Differing perspectives

Many of the disagreements between science and religion could be said to have arisen as a result of unjustified arrogance on one side or the other in relation to their own view of the truth. On the religious side, factual claims were often challenged or defended in the belief that they were crucial to the substance of religious beliefs. Beliefs about the origins of the world and the genesis of human life were cases in point. Scientific discoveries in these areas showed that these beliefs could not be tied too closely to factual claims that were no longer scientifically credible without the danger of embarrassing consequences.

Science thus taught religion that it was unwise to be too presumptuous about the empirical aspects of religious beliefs. As **John Habgood** (1970) put it, 'It is clear that theology ought never to be a competitor with science in the empirical realm. Theological systems are not cosmological hypotheses set up in opposition to scientific cosmology.'

Equally, however, science has had to learn that the demolition of traditional factual assumptions seemingly tied to religious beliefs is not the end of the matter, and certainly not the end of religious faith. In this learning process, science has had to at least grant that the world of empirical fact gives rise to some fair questions. Does this world, for instance, have any overall *meaning* or *significance*? This type of question – a typically *human* question, one might say – is never likely to be answered by the findings of science, as the modern explosion of factual knowledge about the world seems to confirm. The great Spanish thinker **Miguel de Unamuno** (1882–1936) said that man's affective nature craves for a deeper kind of knowledge than the knowledge of empirical facts that science provides. Such craving, he believed, can only ultimately be satisfied by God. The French philosopher **Jacques Maritain** (1882–1973) pointed out that the scepticism begun by Descartes about the world and history has led people to overlook the insights of the history of religion. These show that man has not been able to live by the bread of science alone.

According to Maritain, there are three levels of knowledge: the empirical, the metaphysical and the religious. The shallowest level is the empirical, or scientific. The most profound level is the religious. The mistake, he believed, is to reduce knowledge to the level of the rational, the empirical or even the dogmatic. Knowledge in the truest and fullest sense must go deeper than these levels if it is to satisfy man's deepest needs, which go beyond the earthly and the physical.

**D. C. Goodman**, in *Science and Religious Belief* (1973), has pointed out that the twentieth century has seen a new call for the satisfaction of inner human needs, as well as the reinstatement of human moral values. In neither of these areas does science seem to have much to offer.

The essential nature of religious beliefs is that they are an answer to man's search for meaning and significance in his life. The search for meaning is the search for an *ultimate* explanation of the world. The absence of an ultimate explanation leaves only one alternative, chance. But to posit an ultimate explanation of the world is to presuppose *personal* causality. Personal causality is the essence of a religious explanation of reality.

This idea was already clear to Plato when he put forward the notion of a *World Soul* as the origin of all things. Personal causality is not amenable to scientific investigation. This is because thought, consciousness and will are beyond science. In law, it may be possible to establish that somebody was murdered or robbed, but not *why*. If there is no *why*, there is no purpose. If an occurrence is not the result of impersonal blind forces, it has a purpose, and an explanation that science cannot give – this is the personal.

While this theory of reality is open to challenge, it is not the province of science to do so; nor is it within the competence of scientists *as scientists* to rule it out as illegitimate, since it (a) does not necessarily conflict with science and (b) is logically consistent. Quite simply, either reality is ultimately explicable in terms of purpose or it is not. Religion says that it is. **Keith Ward**, in *Holding Fast to God* (1982), expresses the religious perspective on reality in these words:

> *The world does not run according to mechanistic, purposeless laws. It is consciously directed towards a good end; it realises a purpose, by its very structure and existence. In a real sense, the whole world is the act of God, the expression of his purpose.*

**Michael Polanyi**, in *Personal Knowledge* (1957), reacts strongly to the absence of meaning that is implicit in the scientific view of the universe (see panel).

What is important, of course, is that religion does not put any restrictions on science in its search for the scientific truth about the world. Religion has learned from the past that it is a mistake to tie religious beliefs too closely to seemingly convenient scientific assumptions which may later be shown to be false. **T. H. Huxley**, who styled himself an *agnostic*, saw this tendency as typical of the clericalism of his day. It was the habit of religious leaders (Wilberforce, for example) to reject unwelcome scientific findings (such as evolution) because they appeared to threaten established religious beliefs, of which they considered themselves the guardians. Huxley called clericalism (note, not religion) 'the deadly enemy of science'.

Writing in 1887 on the reception given to Darwin's *The Origin of Species*, he actually said:

> *The doctrine of evolution is neither theistic nor anti-theistic ... It has nothing directly to do with religion ... That which it does collide with is the conception of creation which theologians have based on the story of Genesis ... Genesis is honest to the core, and professes to be no more than it is, a repository of venerable traditions claiming no scientific authority.*

> **PICTURING REALITY**
> *God cannot be observed, any more than truth or beauty can be observed ... all these, like God, are things that can be apprehended only in serving them ...*
>
> *The book of Genesis and its great pictorial illustrations, like the frescoes of Michelangelo, remain a far more intelligent account of the nature and origin of the universe than a representation of the world as a chance collection of atoms. For the biblical cosmology continues to express – however inadequately – the significance of the fact that the world exists and that man has emerged from it, while the scientific picture denies any meaning to the world, and indeed ignores all our most vital experience of this world. The assumption that the world has some meaning which is linked to our own calling as the only morally responsible beings in the world, is an important example of the supernatural aspect of experience which Christian interpretations of the universe explore and develop.*
>
> *Objectivism has totally falsified our conception of truth, by exalting what we can know and prove, while covering up with ambiguous utterances all that we know and cannot prove, even though the latter knowledge underlies, and must ultimately set its seal to, all that we can prove.*
>                                                                    Michael Polanyi

Huxley's experience of clerical opposition to Darwin stands no doubt as a reminder that most disagreements between science and religion are infected with what Pascal said were the *human* realities that taint the search for truth. Whatever the real truth, neither side wants to be put down or made to lose face by the other.

## Changes in the scientific landscape: quantum physics

Religion has had to make important adjustments – and, indeed, concessions – to science in the light of discoveries in the areas of astronomy, geology, biology and cosmology. This has resulted in science believing, with some justification, that its view of truth is clear-sighted and accurate, while religion's view is by comparison unclear and sometimes mistaken. A reversal to this admittedly oversimplified view has taken place in recent years, with discoveries in

# Dimensions of reality

**Scientific view**
Reality is reducible to natural and material processes that have no ultimate significance. Human behaviour will eventually be explained by science

**Religious view**
Reality has many aspects that defy a scientific explanation. The human quest for meaning is evidence of this. Science cannot answer questions that belong to the areas of the *historical*, the *aesthetic*, the *moral* and the *existential*. Religion deals with these typically human dimensions of reality

*To what extent is the scientific view partial and inadequate, using Maritain (p. 78)?*

the microscopic world of quantum physics. Here the confidence of science in establishing facts about the world has been somewhat shaken.

In 1900, **Max Planck** produced quantum mechanics (the physics of the very small) and in 1905 **Albert Einstein** defined relativity (the physics of the very large). The problem is that the two systems are not consistent with each other. **W. Heisenberg's** *indeterminacy principle* (1928) followed from the observation that light can behave either as a *particle* or as a *wave*. The position and momentum of electrons are difficult to identify at once. To allow for the possibility that there could be 'two things at once', **Neils Bohr** (1885–1962) would introduce the *principle of complementarity*.

In simple language, this amounted to a discovery that the objective world is not as easily mapped as was formerly assumed. Theologians could take mild satisfaction from this admission by scientists who had always claimed clarity in their way of speaking, in contrast to theology. For Polkinghorne, the difficulty in dealing with a quantum entity like a light particle 'is not a defect in knowledge, but an insight into the nature of the quantum world'. However, to complicate matters even more, as Polkinghorne points out, an important factor in determining what is 'real' is the viewpoint of the observer.

## Questions about God

It is not a matter of describing accurately an object of knowledge. This is the *correspondence* theory of knowledge, which stresses accuracy and precision in the description of the world. A more adequate and complete account of reality from the human point of view involves the *coherence* theory of knowledge, one which offers a more human, more 'holistic', if sometimes less scientific, account of what is the case. He gives an example:

> *At the material pole of reality, if you split me apart into my constituents, you will just find quarks, and gluons and electrons. Yet you will also have destroyed me. The self resides in the other, holistic, pole of reality.*

In this way of thinking, science only gives a partial view of reality. A more complete view which would take in the realities of *beauty* (the aesthetic), *right and wrong* (the moral) and the *existential* (the search for meaning) would always mean going beyond the purely scientific view of the world. **Albert Einstein** seemed to hint at this when he famously said, 'Religion without science is lame. Science without religion is blind.'

### Einstein

| Religion without science is lame | Science without religion is blind |

*What did Einstein mean?*

## Advances in science: what theology has learned

At this point, it may be useful to bring together some of the lessons that theology has had to learn, and indeed has learned, from the rise of science. Some of these lessons have had the positive effect of clarifying theology's own proper contribution to the understanding of reality.

- Theology can no longer assume, as it once did, that science is a friendly ally. Modern science has asserted itself as an independent area of human inquiry, regardless of its impact on other areas of thought (such as religion).

- Advances in science have helped to clarify how science and theology offer different, but non-conflicting, forms of knowledge about reality.

- Advances in science have helped to establish the priority of science in providing knowledge about how the world is.

- Advances in science have compelled theology to be wary about pronouncing on things which properly belong to the sphere of science.

- Advances in science have led some theologians to see scientific truth as an essential part of theological truth about God and how He works.

- Advances in science have made some theologians more respectful of the difficulties facing scientists in making a place for religious belief.

- Advances in biological science have compelled theologians to undertake a radical revision of their understanding of the biblical story of the origin of life.

- Advances in cosmology have compelled theologians to undertake a similar revision of their understanding of the origin of the world and the cosmos.

- Advances in biology and cosmology have compelled theologians to focus more carefully on how a theological understanding of the world can be integrated with our scientific knowledge.

- Advances in the scientific study of history, and of historical documents, have compelled a revision of how God communicates with man, and how sacred books like the Bible are to be understood.

Advances in science, because of their often challenging nature, have helped to make theology aware of its own proper contribution to the understanding of reality. This must include the recognition that the normal business of theology is to offer *ultimate* explanations of reality as a whole, not *causal* explanations of how events within the world take place.

## Questions about God

Advances in science have, for some theologians, begun to offer the basis of a new natural theology. This is related to (a) the inability of science to go beyond a mere acceptance of the world as a brute fact, or a product of chance and necessity, and (b) its inability to offer a totally satisfying account of man's life, or indeed to offer a solution to the many problems that arise from man's complex emotional, aesthetic and moral (not to mention religious) sensibilities. As Wittgenstein put it, 'We feel that even when all possible scientific questions have been answered the problems of life remain completely untouched.'

### Knowledge

| Scientific | Religious |
| --- | --- |
| The only real knowledge is that which is obtained by the methods of science. Supposed knowledge of things beyond the empirical world is pure speculation – Kant | The nature of man calls for a deeper level of knowledge than that provided by science in order to account for all aspects of life such as beauty, morality, contingency and human spirituality |

*How can Kant be fitted into the right-hand column?*

---

### WAYS OF UNDERSTANDING

*I draw a contrast between two modes of understanding: scientific understanding, which aims to explain the world as it is: and 'intentional understanding', which aims to describe, criticize and justify the world as it appears. The second is an attempt to understand the world in terms of the concepts through which we experience and act on it: these concepts identify the 'intentional objects' of our states of mind. An intentional understanding therefore fills the world with the meanings implicit in our aims and emotions. It tries not so much to explain the world as to be 'at home' in it, recognizing the occasions for action, the objects of sympathy, and the places of rest. The object of such an understanding is not the scientific universe*

> described by scientific theory, but the Lebenswelt, *the world as it is revealed, in and through the life-process which attaches us to it* ...
>
> ... The concepts which inform our emotions bear the stamp of a shared human interest, and of a constantly developing form of life. Whence do they come? ... These concepts are the gift of culture, being neither consciously made nor deliberately chosen but evolved over generations. It is by the use of such concepts of good and evil, sacred and profane, tragic and comic, just and unjust – all of them rooted in that one vital idea which, I would contend, denotes no natural kind, and conveys a classification that could feature in no true scientific theory of man: the concept of the person. The concepts of a culture classify the world in terms of the appropriate action and the appropriate response. A rational being has need of such concepts, which bring his emotions together in the object, so enabling him – as the Hegelians would say – to find his identity *in* the world and not in opposition to it. A culture, moreover, is essentially shared; its concepts and images bear the mark of participation, and are intrinsically consoling, in the manner of a religious communion, or an act of worship. They close again the gap between the subject and object which yawns so frighteningly in the world of science.
>
> Estrangement from the world is the poisoned gift of science.
> 
> Roger Scruton (1990)

## Theology since evolution

If evolution is taken to be one of the great landmarks in the recent history of science, it is probably true to say that its arrival also marked a decisive turning-point for theology. One noticeable effect of the rise of science was to make theology more aware of its empirical claims. This can easily be seen at the critical level. Empirical suppositions about such things as the age of the earth, the origins of life, the nature of the universe and even the formation of the Bible were drastically revised following the application of modern science. Theology had to surrender its claims to be an authority in matters of empirical truth, and give way to science.

At another level, theology has begun to take science on in its own terms. It has done this by turning to the empirical world to raise anew old questions associated with natural theology. The empirical world, including human existence, contains features that call for an explanation. This approach is implied in **John Wisdom's** parable of the garden (see Chapter 4). In the parable, the believer looks to features of the garden (the world) that support belief in a gardener (God).

Empirically based considerations have also come to the fore in connection with the so-called *anthropic principle* (from the Greek *anthropos*, meaning man). In its most basic form – sometimes called the 'weak' version – the anthropic principle means no more than the observation that the universe must have produced the conditions needed for human consciousness to evolve. Otherwise, we would not *be* here in the first place. The 'strong' version of the principle holds that the universe was designed with the ultimate purpose of producing human life. Thus the strong anthropic principle entails religious belief in a divine creator.

Recently, **John Polkinghorne**, in *Scientists as Theologians* (1996), has put forward what he calls a 'moderate anthropic principle'. This is the more modest claim that a universe which has produced life is a 'fact of interest calling for an explanation' precisely because of the constellation of conditions required for the emergence of life, let alone human life.

As an illustration of the unlikely, Polkinghorne uses the rather poor example of a fly on a large blank wall, being hit by a stray bullet. For Polkinghorne, the anthropic principle calls attention to the unlikelihood of human life being the result of blind chance. It gives rise to 'considerations to which theism provides a persuasive (but not logically coercive) answer'. More tellingly, he says, 'I have seen the anthropic principle as being a component in a *revised and revived form of natural theology*' (my emphasis).

In other words, chance and necessity stretch the imagination too much to offer a credible explanation for the way the universe is 'fine tuned' to produce life. In *Beyond Science* (1996), Polkinghorne appears to draw a more explicitly theistic conclusion: 'I believe ... anthropic considerations are ... part of a cumulative case for theism ... I believe that in the delicate fine-tuning of physical law, which has made the evolution of conscious beings possible, we receive a valuable, if indirect, hint from science that there is a divine meaning and purpose behind cosmic history.'

# The anthropic principle

**Scientific**
That we are here to observe the universe may be remarkable, but is merely a brute fact

**Religious**
The wonder that we are here to observe the universe, against the odds of life emerging at all, makes a religious response fitting

*What is Polkinghorne's 'moderate' anthropic principle?*

Another modern thinker who believes that science can be harmonised with faith – and, indeed, used to confirm it – is the German theologian **Wolfhart Pannenberg**. In *Jesus: God and Man* (1968), Pannenberg rejected attempts by Barth and Bultmann to evade the threat of science by making theology and history, respectively, immune to scientific investigation (see Chapter 4, Rudolf Bultmann). **Barth** tried to do this by his 'retreat to the citadel', proclaiming faith to be a special insight into religious history, regardless of what secular science might discover. **Bultmann** believed that the data of faith lay beyond the scope of scientific investigation (particularly by the science of history).

Attempts to discover the historical truth of the gospel stories surrounding Jesus were both futile and inappropriate for faith. It was far better to see the whole gospel as a call to a higher level of *existence*. The true meaning of the story of Jesus is its *existential significance* for man's life in the world, the secret of which is its revelation of what it means to achieve *authentic existence* (that is, salvation). For Pannenberg, these approaches were an evasion. We actually know enough from *history* to be certain of the truths of faith.

Central to Pannenberg's argument is the Resurrection of Jesus. This was an event open to non-religious (secular) and purely historical *scientific* investigation. Set against the background of its time (expectation of the end of the world), and confirmed by empirical evidence (the empty tomb and the conviction of the Apostles), the Resurrection of Jesus was an event, not of *salvation history* as Barth had held, but of *universal history*.

Does this mean that faith is at the mercy of history? Pannenberg's daring approach means 'yes'. Faith can be shown to be soundly based on rational evidence from the *past*. But it still requires a religious commitment for the *future*. As a Lutheran, Pannenberg still holds that *fiducia*, or trust, is required that God will be faithful in extending Christ's fate to us. In a compliment to Pannenberg, the *Blackwell Encyclopedia of Christian Thought* (1993) said that 'his programme is likely to be of considerable interest for some time to come'.

Other theologians have sought to preserve the place of religion by emphasising how faith is concerned with a transcendent, non-empirical reality, unlike anything in the world of science. As a result, they have attempted to move away from concern with *facts*, whether they be the facts of science or the facts of history. God is not some objective empirical reality 'out there', whose existence is another 'fact' available to investigation, but a mystery that cannot be objectified or spoken about. God is real nevertheless. His reality is perceived in ways which are, admittedly, unlike our perception of empirical things, but are intelligible enough to bring meaning and significance for human life and existence. Expressions such as the 'death of God' (Nietzsche), the 'ground of our being' (Tillich), 'Being Itself' (Macquarrie) and 'Absolute Horizon' (Rahner) have provided the background and framework for a new non-empirical understanding of God among some modern theologians (see Chapter 4, New ideas of God).

# Chapter 3 | God and Experience

In the first two chapters, we have been concerned with the question of God's existence, largely from the point of view of reason. In Chapter 1, we looked at the philosophical problems of proving or establishing God's existence. In Chapter 2, we looked at the impact of modern science on Christian belief. We can say that one of the main questions up to now has been: 'Can God's existence be inferred from, or be consistent with, the nature of the world?'

In this chapter, we shall examine the claim that God can be the direct object of experience. This is a claim that underlies much of the Bible, and has continued to be made by believers down the centuries. This claim that God can be *directly* experienced will be distinguished from, but is not unrelated to, the claim that God can be grasped at certain moments through aspects of *ordinary everyday* experience. But first we turn to the Bible.

One of the basic assumptions of the Bible is that God both can be experienced and, indeed, *has* been experienced by human beings. Much of the story of the *Old Testament* may be said to hinge around certain direct encounters between individuals and God. This assumption underlies the encounters between God and Noah, God and Abraham, and God and Moses, to name but a few. We shall single out for inspection one of the most dramatic and colourful encounters recorded in the Bible – that between God and Moses, described in Exod. 3.1–6:

> *Moses was looking after the flock of Jethro, his father in law, priest of Midian. He led his flock to the far side of the wilderness and came to Horeb, the mountain of God. There the angel of Yahweh appeared to him in the shape of a flame of fire, coming from the middle of a bush. Moses looked; there was the bush blazing but it was not being burned up. 'I must go and look at this strange sight', Moses said, 'and see why the bush is not burned'. Now Yahweh saw him go forward to look, and God called to him from the middle of the bush. 'Moses, Moses', he said. 'Here*

## Questions about God

God in the burning bush, from the twelfth-century church of Panagia, Asinou, Cyprus

> I am', he answered. 'Come no nearer', he said. 'Take off your shoes, for the place on which you stand is holy ground. I am the God of your father', he said, 'the God of Abraham, the God of Isaac and the God of Jacob'. At this Moses covered his face, afraid to look at God.

At no time, it must be said, does the Bible deal with the philosophical or epistemological problem of how, if God speaks or appears, the recipient knows that it is God. It would be beyond the scope of this study to go into this complex question. Whatever the exact nature of Moses' experience, history testifies to the effect that it had on him. We can take it that he was convinced that he had encountered God. Philosophically, if God exists, there is no logical difficulty in his existence being the possible object of experience – whatever form it may take.

In the *New Testament*, there is a noticeable change in the understanding of how God communicates with man. Here the focus of interest shifts from God to the person of Jesus Christ. The theological reason for this is given in Mark 9.7–8: 'And a cloud came covering them in shadow; and there came a voice from the cloud, "This is my Son, the Beloved. Listen to him." ' It is given later, in Hebrews 1.1–2: 'At various times in the past, and in various different ways, God spoke to our ancestors through the prophets; but in our own time, the last days, he has spoken to us through his Son ...'

These passages help to explain why the life and teaching of Jesus was seen by the Church as the final revelation of God to man (see Chapter 1, Revelation). What is significant is the *manner* of this revelation. No longer is it by way of dramatic experiences, as in the case of Moses. Now it is through an ordinary human life. As **Gabriel Moran** has put it, in *Theology of Revelation* (1967), 'It is now through the veil of human flesh that God is revealed. The revelation takes place not in terms of words or a message but through the manifestation of a person.' Since the Church was now the official guardian of revelation, personal religious experience of the kind attributed to Moses tended to be regarded with suspicion, and was seen as a possible threat to its authority. Besides, the New Testament itself seemed to downplay religious experience as a basis for faith. Jesus said to Thomas: 'Blessed are they who have not seen and yet have believed' (John 20.29). Paul said that 'we walk by faith, not by sight' (2 Cor. 5.7).

Yet claims of religious experience would feature prominently in the history of the Christian faith. Not surprisingly, many religious experiences would now centre on Jesus as the manifestation of God. But claims of religious experience would take many forms. First, we must look at the different meanings given to the term 'religious experience'.

A twelfth-century image of the Holy Face, from the Tretyakov Gallery, Moscow. Religious experience was not a gospel promise. Jesus would later become the focus of many claims of religious experience

# I RELIGIOUS EXPERIENCE: DIRECT AND INDIRECT

The term 'religious experience' has many meanings, ranging from a perceived direct encounter with the divine, or God, to a feeling or sense of the divine that is somehow perceived within ordinary everyday experience. Direct experience of the divine is a claim made by many individuals, and is classically exemplified by those encounters with God described in the Bible. Claims of a direct perception of God have also been central to the so-called mystical tradition, and such claims have continued to be made by countless people down the ages. Intense experiences of these kinds usually lead to a deepening of religious faith, and sometimes to a dramatic *conversion* of life (see below).

A less dramatic and more indirect experience of the divine is said to be perceptible within ordinary experience, and is held by some to depend on the development of a special faculty of apprehension or appreciation, somewhat parallel to our capacity to appreciate art or music. This understanding of religious experience is the one we find expressed in the writings of **F. D. E. Schleiermacher** (see below). He claimed that we all have a sense, or feeling, of total *dependence* if only we stop to reflect on it. He called it 'a sense of absolute dependence'. This is a basic intuition that we are all capable of developing, and it lies deeper than the level of rational thinking. It is this intuition which gives us an awareness of the reality of God and religion.

A more specific form of awareness – more directly religious – is analysed by **Rudolf Otto** (1869–1937) in *The Idea of the Holy* (1923). Otto rejected the current idea that religion was an historical or sociological phenomenon. Instead, he argued, it was rooted in a personal experience of what he called the *numinous* (taken from a distinction used by Kant – the *phenomenon* is the empirical, while the *numenon* is beyond the empirical). We are capable of perceiving the numinous as a *mysterious* but real object of experience. This experience, says Otto, evokes awe and wonder, and is at once fearsome and fascinating, provoking attraction and repulsion at the same time. This perception of the holy is not the result of rational thinking or reasoning, but is a form of direct intuition. Otto gives as an example the feeling that came over people after a storm destroyed a partially built bridge on the Rhine. When the storm abated, an eerie silence descended on the river, evoking a strange sense of awe and fear at the power of nature. For Otto, the experience of the numinous, or the *holy*, lay at the root of all religions. Whether his under-

*God and Experience*

Could a sense of the numinous, or the holy, be gained from certain places, such as this ruined cloister in Ireland? Is faith a prerequisite for such an experience?

standing of the numinous amounts to a direct or indirect experience of God remains open to discussion.

**David Hay**, in his book *Religious Experience Today* (1990), appears to go beyond Otto when he uses the term *numinous* to describe a more specific experience of God which many people claim to have. Such experiences are often expressed in terms of 'I knew God was there' or 'I felt I was in the presence of God'. **J. C. A. Gaskin**, in *The Quest for Eternity* (1984), however, distinguishes between numinous *religious* experience (direct experience of the divine) and numinous experience of a more general kind.

He illustrates the latter with a quotation from **Albert Einstein**: 'The fairest thing we can experience is the mysterious ... a knowledge of the existence of something we cannot penetrate ... it is this knowledge and this emotion that constitute the truly religious attitude.' This seems closer to what Otto called the numinous. But, as Gaskin points out, such experiences may not be interpreted by everyone as religious. These kinds of feelings are sometimes called 'depth' or 'peak' experiences, and are often found expressed in poetry and literature. Gaskin calls them by the name 'numinous agnostic' to indicate that they may not necessarily be linked to religion. **David Hay** describes them as feelings which give rise to a sense of 'merging' with the rest of reality. In a general sense, he calls these 'mystical' experiences, and their recipients 'nature mystics'.

**William James** (1842–1910) saw religion as essentially based on experience. He defined religion as 'the feelings, acts and experiences of individual men in their solitude, so far as they apprehend themselves to stand in relation to whatever they may consider the divine'. Here James identifies an important aspect of religious experience, namely that it is usually a *solitary* experience of an individual alone. (The phenomenon of group religious experiences raises important questions that lie outside the scope of this study.)

Because of the many forms that religious experience can take, **Ninian Smart**, in *The Religious Experience of Mankind* (1969), like James, describes it in very general terms:

> *A religious experience involves some kind of 'perception' of the invisible world, or a perception that some visible person or thing is a manifestation of the invisible world.*

We can see, then, that the term 'religious experience' is capable of different interpretations. Broadly speaking, and allowing for some grey areas, it can be divided into claims of *direct* experience of the divine or God, and claims of *indirect* experience of God through aspects of ordinary experience.

In the following sections, we shall now look at some of the more specific forms that religious experiences have taken in the lives of people, beginning with conversions.

## Conversion experiences

In *The Varieties of Religious Experience*, William James (1901) says

> *To be converted, to be regenerated, to receive grace, to experience religion, to gain an assurance, are so many phrases which denote the process,*

> gradual or sudden, by which a self, hitherto divided, and consciously wrong, inferior and unhappy, becomes unified and consciously right, superior and happy, in consequence of its firmer hold upon religious realities.
> ...
>
> To say a man is 'converted' means, in these terms, that religious ideas, previously peripheral in his consciousness, now take a central place, and that religious aims form the habitual centre of his energy.

### Paul of Tarsus (d. ad 60)
Paul's own account of his conversion is described in Acts 22.1–21:

> I am a Jew ... and was ... zealous for God. I persecuted the followers of this Way to their death ... At about noon I came near Damascus, suddenly a bright light from heaven flashed around me. I fell to the ground and heard a voice say to me, 'Saul! Saul! Why do you persecute me?' 'Who are you Lord?', I asked. 'I am Jesus of Nazareth, whom you are persecuting',* he replied. My companions saw the light, but they did not understand the voice of him who was speaking to me. 'What shall I do Lord?', I asked. 'Get up', the Lord said, 'and go into Damascus. There you will be told all that you have been assigned to do.'

\* In Acts 26.14, Jesus adds the words 'it is hard for you to kick against the goads' (see p. 96).

### Assessment of Paul's conversion
Paul's conversion does not fit James's description of religious conversion in one important respect. Paul (previously called Saul) was in fact already a religious man – fanatically so, it seems. Paul was a practising Jew, and looked on Christians (followers of the Way) as enemies. Where Paul's conversion does fit James's description is in the effect that it had on him. Paul became a changed man, full of zeal and energy for the new life to which his conversion led. He would become one of the outstanding figures in the founding of the Christian Church, and would die for his faith.

Paul's conversion was an historical fact. But what of the event itself? Was it as miraculous as the account suggests? The answer is open to speculation. James considers the possibility that conversion experiences may have *psychological* explanations, involving both conscious and subconscious elements, although these would not necessarily rule out a divine influence. The psychologist **C. G. Jung** has offered the theory that Paul's conversion was the outcome of a personal crisis about which he felt guilty and did not want to admit; namely, his hatred of Christians. The event on the road to Damascus was the result of being overwhelmed by guilt. This created a state of physical and emotional turmoil (he fell to the ground and was later blind). This was followed by a resolution of the crisis. The words of Jesus in Acts 26 (see above) may lend support to this view.

Such theories are legitimate speculation, and are an attempt to throw light on what was a very extraordinary event. A natural explanation of the kind put forward by Jung would not necessarily rule out a *religious* explanation. God may well work through natural processes, including emotional and psychological ones. But for **Richard Swinburne**, in *Is there a God?* (1996), however much we may surmise about what happened, it is the subject of the experience who is best placed to interpret its meaning.

Using the *principle of credulity*, he says 'Religious perceptual claims deserve to be taken as seriously as perceptual claims of any other kind.' It is of course central to conversion experiences that the subject interprets them as religious experiences, with religious consequences (see also the examples of Augustine and Wesley). In any case, there is no inherent inconsistency between a psychological and a more directly religious interpretation. What may be objected to is a *reductive* interpretation, which 'reduces' the event in question to a merely psychological happening. As will be seen below, this kind of reductionism will be central to atheistic interpretations of religious claims.

---

AUGUSTINE OF HIPPO (AD 354–430)

Augustine of Hippo, later St Augustine, was to become one of the most influential leaders and theologians of the early Church. The turning-point of his life was a moment of conversion which he describes in his *Confessions*. It happened in a garden on a hot summer's day in the company of an old friend. He was in a state of emotional distress and in tears when he heard the voice of a child coming from a nearby building telling him 'take up and read' – whereupon his eyes fell on the words of St Paul: 'put ye on the Lord Jesus Christ, and make not provision for the flesh in concupiscence' (Rom.13.14). His old friend Alypius, who was with him, had a similar experience. Both felt new men, full of assurance, strength and peace. It was a remarkable conversion for Augustine. He had lived a dissolute and wayward life, which he now left behind – and he went on to become a saint. Human factors certainly played a part. His mother, St Helena, was already a Christian, and through contact with people such as St Ambrose, bishop of Milan, he had taken a keen interest in the Bible and Christian teachings. Significantly, he had also known about the conversion of St Anthony of Egypt (251–351) who, when he read the words of Mark 10.21, felt that they were addressed to him. For these reasons Augustine's conversion cannot exactly be said to have happened out of the blue.

## JOHN WESLEY (1703–1791)

As the son of a rector, John Wesley was brought up as a devout Christian. As a student at Oxford he took religion seriously, and tried to apply its teachings about concern for others. After ordination in 1725, he went to America as a missionary, where he came in contact with German Pietists. He began to be preoccupied with his spiritual state, believing that he was not fully justified in God's sight. The Moravian pietist Perter Mohler advised him to stop worrying, and to 'preach faith till you have it'. After much searching, and even despair, there came a sudden moment of enlightenment. It was triggered by his reading of Ps. 130, and the first chapter of 2 Peter. Later, he read Luther's account of how God works in the heart through faith. He said, 'I felt my heart strangely warmed ... and an assurance was given to me that [Christ] had taken away my sins.' Wesley openly testified to how he now felt, although he would later admit to a 'lack of joy'. Neverthless, the conversion remained, and changed his life.

At this point, we can identify four stages in the conversion process:

1 prior interest in religious questions and other related issues

2 the influence of other cases of conversion (see Augustine and Wesley above)

3 a crisis situation, involving physical and emotional upset

4 the moment of conversion, bringing about a radical change in feeling and outlook

## Mystical experience

'Mysticism' is the name given to the experience of oneness or union with the divine, spoken of by many saints and believers. The word *mystic* comes from the Greek, meaning *to close*, and was used in connection with the lips or the mind. **Margaret Smith** (1961) says that the word 'mystic' implies secrecy, and came to be associated with the closing of the mind to external distractions in order to receive divine illumination. She quotes an oriental scholar: 'Mysticism is an aspiration of the soul to cease altogether from self and be at one with God ... it is a tendency of the human soul for unity with God ... it is begotten of love not self-interest.'

According to **Hans Kung**, in *Does God Exist?: an Answer for Today* (1980), mysticism is characterised by a closing of the senses to the external world, and a dissolving of the self. The aim is to seek salvation in the depths of one's own soul, through a form of intercourse or union with God. Kung believes that mysticism tends to develop in reaction to institutionalised religion which puts the emphasis on the externals of religion, such as ritual and sacrament. By contrast, mysticism stresses the *individual* religious sense. It may be significant that many, although not all, of the great mystics have come from within the Catholic tradition, where there is strong emphasis on *communal* worship and ritual.

There are four presuppositions of mysticism:

1 there is an inner capacity for direct intuition of the divine

2 God is the ground of the soul (as the spark is to the flame)

3 Only by purification of the self can union be achieved

4 The ultimate guiding principle of the mystic is love, not self-seeking

*The mystic way*
This was classified by **St Bonaventure** (1221–1274), the teacher of Thomas Aquinas. He saw mystical experience as having three stages:

1 in the *purgative* stage, the mystic is prepared and purified by prayer and discipline (or asceticism)

2 in the *illuminative* stage, the mystic enjoys an experience which is emotionally and spiritually illuminating

3 in the final, or *unitive* stage, the mystic enjoys a sense of oneness with God

## The mystic way

| St Bonaventure's three stages of the mystic way | Purgative<br>Illuminative<br>Unitive |
|---|---|

*Which is the easiest stage to verify?*

*The mystical tradition*
**Dionysius the Areopagite** (AD 500) is generally regarded as one of the first great Christian mystics, although the mystical tradition itself is rooted in the Bible. Dionysius was influenced by neo-Platonism, which created the distinction between the world of sense and the invisible world of 'ideal Forms'. The latter is the real world. By comparison, the visible world of the senses is only a shadow. The Form of the Good is the ultimate reality. This later came to be identified with God. Only by the practice of virtue and self-denial (asceticism) can the soul achieve its true destiny, union with the Good.

## Questions about God

The ideas of Plato were revived by **Plotinus** (205–270), an Egyptian philosopher. He identified love as 'the activity of the soul desiring the Good'. Since God is the highest Good, it is natural that the soul should strive towards Him in love. This involves a process of self-purification and training. These ideas formed the basis of later mysticism. One of the problems that Dionysius tried to grapple with was the problem of communicating, or describing, mystical experience. The problem lay in the peculiar nature of mystical experience. It is not an experience of anything in particular, since it appears to have no distinct object. **William James** noted that the descriptions of mystics were more akin to music than to conceptual speech, with frequent use of paradoxes, such as 'whispering silence', 'dazzling obscurity' or 'teeming desert'.

James said that 'mysticism is a wide field of experience which is inclusive of many experiences at once ... the whole of reality is uncovered at once and seen as one'. Elsewhere, he calls mystical states *windows* into a more inclusive world. For James, mystical states had four charactistics:

1 *ineffability* – words are unable to describe their contents

2 they have a *noetic* quality; in other words, they are states of knowledge, not just emotional experiences – they bring new insights, beyond what the intellect can grasp

3 they are markedly *transient* – they cannot be sustained for long at a time

4 in the mystical state the subject is *passive*, in the sense of being overwhelmed by the experience

## The mystical experience (James)

| Characteristics of mystical states | Ineffable |
| | Noetic |
| | Transient |
| | Objective |

*What problems are raised by these four aspects of mystical experience?*

## God and Experience

In his book *The Foundations of Mysticism* (1992), **Bernard McGinn** finds significance in the distinction made by Dionysius between two kinds of knowing. There is the knowing by mental and intellectual effort (mathein), and knowing by direct experience (pathein), terms borrowed from Aristotle. Mysticism is associated with the latter. There is also the distinction between the ineffable and mysterious on the one hand, and the open and more evident on the other. Here, mysticism is associated with the former. For Dionysius, to speak of God was to stretch language to the limit. Of mysticism, he said: 'What is to be said of it remains unsayable; what is to be understood of it remains unknowable.' But he provided later mystics with a key by which they could try to unlock the secrets of their experiences, while at the same time show the complexity of attempting to do so.

We shall return below to some of the problems raised by mysticism and religious experience.

---

WHAT MYSTICS HAVE SAID

*Human language is unable to express the sense of mystical union with God.*

St John of the Cross

*The mystical experience leaves the subject absolutely convinced of its reality.*

*In the orison of union the soul is fully awake as regards God, but wholly asleep as regards things of this world and in respect of herself ... thus does God, when he raises a soul to union with Himself, suspend the natural action of all her faculties.*

*Our Lord made me comprehend in what way it is that one God can be in three persons. He made me see it so clearly that I was as surprised as I was comforted.*

*The soul which becomes one with God who gives Himself in love, cannot but give itself to others in love.*

St Teresa of Avila

> *God may be loved but not thought.*
> from the Cloud of Unknowing, anon.
>
> *Mysticism includes activity for a whole life.*
> Ruysbroeck
>
> *The vision is not of God, Person or Spirit, but of oneness.*
>
> *If Christ became man ... man can become Christ and hence become God ... but only through detachment and self-abandonment.*
> Meister Eckhart
>
> *God is unknowable, beyond any creature to know ... enough to know that He is ... and knowing this to love Him and rejoice in Him, and rest in Him.*
> Richard Rolle
>
> *And he showed me more, a little thing, the size of a hazelnut, on the palm of my hand, round like a ball. I looked at it thoughtfully and wondered, 'What is this?' And the answer came, 'It is all that is made.' I marvelled. It exists, both now and forever, because God loves it.*
> Julian of Norwich

---

## MEISTER ECKHART (1260–1329)

Regarded today as one of the giants in the history of mysticism, Eckhart ended his life under a cloud, having been condemned by the Pope for his unorthodox views. Although a mystic of profound spiritual insight, he combined his mysticism with an aggressive commitment to social justice: 'The person who understands what I have to say about justice understands everything I have to say.' He was also an outstanding champion of womens' rights, and of the spirtual dignity of the peasant classes. Eckhart rejected the established three-fold path of mysticism of purgation, illumination and union, and replaced it with his own *Four Ways*:

> 1  The *via positiva*. This was centred on the recognition of God's presence in everything. 'God is a great underground river that no one can dam up and no one can stop', he said.
>
> 2  The *via negativa*. God is the 'not-person, not-thing ... the nameless nothingness and superessential darkness.' The secret of union with God was in letting go of material things, not because they were bad, but because we tend to cling to them. 'Where clinging ends is where God begins.'
>
> 3  The *via creativa* involves the recognition that we are meant to be co-creators with God, not passive observers of life. In our creativity lies all blessings.
>
> 4  The *via transformativa* involves the recognition that all created things are interdependent. This calls for compassion, a natural sympathy with all fellow beings. Until God works compassion in us, we do not have a soul. But its first form must be justice: 'For the just person as such, to act justly is to live; indeed, justice is his life, his being alive, his being ... if our being is just our works will be.'

## Assessment of religious experience

At this point, we may pause to consider some of the issues that arise in connection with claims for direct religious experience, including mysticism. A further assessment will form part of our consideration of atheistic interpretations of religion (and hence of religious experience) below.

**William James** held an open mind about claims of religious experience. He accepted that these claims were highly subjective, and carried no authority for those who have not had such experience. Yet he was convinced that in its purest form (free of what he called 'useless excesses') it brought distinct benefits to the recipients. He said that the best examples 'are characterised by optimism ... they are reconciling and unifying, deriving from an experience of God as the transcendent and unlimited'. Such experiences also brought benefits to society. 'The best fruits of religious experiences are the best things that history has to show.'

James was especially impressed by the close connection between mysticism and *saintliness*. He disagreed with **Nietzsche** that saints were 'sick'. Saints showed a concern for the rooting out of selfishness, and the love of God. For the saints, this also meant the love of others. This explains why saints have always been valued within society. An implication of this would be that religious experience, being an important source of saintliness, must also be valued. Support for this view comes from an unexpected source. The atheist **Emile Durkheim** (1915) observed that 'the believer who has communicated with his God is not merely a man who sees new truths of which the unbeliever is ignorant; he is a man who is stronger'.

The psychologist **Carl G. Jung** (1958) was impressed by the healing effects of such experience. 'Religious experience is absolute ... it cannot be disputed. Those who have had it possess a great treasure, a source of life, meaning and beauty which gives a new splendour to the world. It is overwhelming and healing and is therefore of great validity.'

Religious experience, however, remains problematic because of its highly individualistic and private nature. As **A. Harrison-Barbet** in *The Philosophy of Religion* (1990) has pointed out, there is always the possibility of alternative explanations, of delusion and deception, and the difficulty of establishing objective criteria to judge the experience. **Bertrand Russell** expressed, with typical wit, the modern atheistic scepticism about religious experience: 'From a scientific point of view we can make no distinction between the man who eats little and sees heaven and the man who drinks much and sees snakes.' The key word here is of course 'scientific'. It would be difficult to imagine how any inner experience (including dreams) could come within the range of scientific investigation. Nevertheless, there are serious issues involved in claims to religious experience. To these we now turn.

## Problems of religious experience

The problems connected with religious experience may be categorised under two headings: *theological* and *philosophical*. We begin with a look at the theological problems raised by religious experience, and by mysticism in particular. The philosophical problems will be considered in the section that follows.

## Theological objections

As we suggested above, the idea of private access to God outside the official channels of prayer, worship and the reading of scripture has never been greatly encouraged by the official Church. Mystics have never received more than cautious approval by Church authorities, because of the fundamental principle that God's revelation has come definitively through Jesus Christ, and that the Church is the official guardian of that revelation. This is not unusual. In most large organisations, communication is carefully controlled, and is usually restricted to official spokespersons. Whenever there are claims of special inner experiences, there is often the danger of delusion and fanaticism. For these reasons, mystical and other claims of direct experience of God are scrutinised strictly by the Church.

Another problem with mysticism is the idea that it suggests some kind of favouritism on the part of God. Mystics often appear to be an elite group, given favoured access to the experience of God. It may be argued, however, that mystics simply respond better than other people to the opportunity to experience God. The fact that mystics go to considerable lengths to get into the mystic state (see The mystic way, above) lends credence to this view. Only those who make the effort are the ones who take the opportunity to experience God, an opportunity that is open to everyone.

**Robert Way**, in *The Wisdom of the English Mystics* (1978), supports this view by pointing out that mysticism is often a costly experience. Despite great efforts and dedication, some of the well known mystics of the past often suffered long periods of profound dereliction (for example, St John of the Cross spoke of 'the dark night of the soul'), while their mystical experiences were relatively brief.

On the other hand, mystics could be said to have given as much as they have received. Mystics have been valued within the Church for the way they have helped to bring new insights into well-known beliefs, such as the meaning of Christ's passion and death, the reality of forgiveness and the love of God. However, their mystical experiences bring no new knowledge about God that is not available to others. **Aquinas** had said that mystical experience was an experience *of* God, not *about* God. The Catholic theologian **R. Garrigou-Lagrange** disagreed that mystics could be called an elite. He said: 'mysticism is the full flowering of the ordinary life of grace *open to all Christians*' (my emphasis). The **Second Vatican**

**Council** (1962) reflected this view when it declared that mysticism was part of the *general call to holiness*, and was in principle a grace available to all.

## Philosophical problems

Claims about the inner origins of private and personal experience are notoriously difficult to establish. **Descartes** famously doubted even experience itself. Loss of confidence in experience as a basis of knowledge of the world led him to seek certainty in the clear and distinct ideas of *reason*. He said he could never be sure whether he was dreaming or awake! **Thomas Hobbes** (1588–1679) asked what was the difference between saying 'God spoke to me in a dream' and 'I dreamt that God spoke to me'. With this question, Hobbes identified the problem of verifying the origins of inner experience, and anticipated the modern empiricist challenge to religious beliefs and assertions.

The problem also becomes one of communication. This is typically stated by **A. J. Ayer**: 'If a mystic admits that the object of his vision is something which cannot be described, then he must also admit that he is bound to talk nonsense when he describes it ... in describing his vision the mystic does not give us any information about the external world; he merely gives us indirect information about the condition of his own mind.' In these words, Ayer is expressing the classic logical positivist criticism of religious claims, and the language used to express them (see Chapter 4). All that can be said at this stage is that the mystical tradition has had a reputable history, and many mystics have been individuals of undoubted balance and integrity. **William James** said that mysticism was not 'a sign of a degenerate brain'. For this reason, their claims cannot so easily be dismissed on the technicalities of language, as Ayer appears to do.

However, in the final analysis, is religious experience what the recipient says it is? Is it an experience of the divine or of God? James avoids this question on the grounds that it cannot ultimately be settled. He prefers to take a pragmatic approach – if such experiences 'work' for an individual, that is more important than any question about their origin. But is this not a case of sacrificing truth to utility? Because something is useful, does that make it true? As a pragmatist, James would consider beneficial effects to be more important than the question of their origin. For this reason, he pursues the question no further.

**John Bowker**, in *The Sense of God* (1973), takes a slightly different line. He argues that the criterion for judging claims to inner knowledge is not some rationally agreed yardstick, which is often expressed in terms of empirical verification. Rather, the criterion is *sincerity* or *authenticity*. In other words, the honesty of the recipient is the best clue to the truth of their claims. If this is so, then many of the claims for mystical experience have considerable weight. **William Alston**, in *Perceiving God: the Epistemology of Religious Experience* (1991), seeks to establish the credibility of religious experience by linking it to other arguments for God's existence. In his view, if God exists, the idea of a direct experience of God is not improbable. As in the case of miracles, there is no logical reason why God couldn't reveal Himself directly – as, indeed, exemplified in the Bible.

## Forms of religious experience

Visions (Moses, Jesus)
Conversions (Paul, Augustine)
Mystical union (Dionysius)
Sense of dependence (Schleiermacher)
Sense of the holy (Otto)
Sense of the personal (Buber)
Sense of the mysterious (nature poets etc.)
Sense of the transcendent (Rahner)

*What are the similarities and differences between these various forms?*

## Indirect religious experience

The more general kind of religious experience arising, for instance, from the sense of absolute dependence spoken of by **Schleiermacher**, does not present the same problems as claims of a direct experience of God. This former kind of experience, it can be argued, is a universal human capacity which makes it possible to see a religious aspect within ordinary experience. This view is held by **John Hick**, who sees religious experience as a matter of interpreting ordinary experience in a way that leads to a sense of God's presence or activity. God is thus perceived indirectly through the experience.

## Questions about God

Can seeing God in nature be called a valid religious experience?

It is difficult to see how this can be any more than the normal functioning of religious faith, which provides a perspective on how the believer sees the world (see the parables in Chapter 4). The problem with this view is that it tends to confine religious experience to a *psychological* reaction, leaving little else to justify calling it a religious experience.

On the other hand, **C. S. Evans** in *Thinking about Faith* (1982) has introduced the idea of *mediated* experiences of God, which he calls *direct*. He gives the example of a person hearing the voice of God through a sermon or a hymn. Here, he seems to come close to Hick's view, but his claim is more objective. He argues that since God is the Creator of the world, everything in it is capable of mediating God directly. Evans, however, fails to show that a mediated experience is any more than a subjective or personal reaction.

We conclude this section by considering some of the questions raised by the particular kind of religious experience called a 'miracle'.

*God and Experience*

## Miracles

**St Augustine** stated the traditional understanding of a miracle, as 'an event we cannot forecast or expect with our present understanding of nature'. This reflects the view that miracles are somehow violations of the laws of nature, and presupposes that God is the only power who can do this. **Aquinas** defines miracles as 'things which are done by divine agency beyond the order commonly observed in nature'.

**Brian Davies**, in *Thinking About God* (1985), believes that a wider definition of the miracle is now more common. Miracles are 'unexpected and fortuitous events in the light of which we are disposed to give thanks to God'. The word 'fortuituous' leaves open the possibility that the event is normal, but is *perceived* as showing the hand of God. One of the miracle windows of Canterbury Cathedral illustrates such an event. A man is buried alive in a tunnel and his workmates go for help. In the meantime, his distant cries are heard by a passing traveller and he is saved. In the background, a hand can be seen emerging from a cloud, indicating that the event was a miracle.

## Experience and belief

To what extent does our experience determine what we believe, and what we believe determine what we experience?

*How can this be applied to the understanding of miracles?*

This view of miracles, as events *seen* as bearing the hand of God, has been popularised by **John Hick**. He believes that many of the Old Testament miracles, such as the plagues of Egypt and the crossing of the Red Sea, were probably natural occurrences which happened so fortuituously that they were seen as miracles caused by God. A similar view is taken by the so-called *Process theologians* (see Chapter 4). They see God's action as permanently immanent in the world. This makes the idea of God's intervention from outside untenable. Agreeing with **Rudolf Bultmann** that in the scientific age it is no longer possible to believe in 'direct divine intrusion into the field of human events', **Donald Neil**

(1984) finds it significant that all the biblical miracles, especially those of Jesus, involved the mediation or action of a human being. This shows that God's action in the world is not an intrusion from outside, but is done through human agency *from within*.

This view is also shared by **John Habgood**, in an article entitled 'God's action in the world' (1991). He believes that the action of God in the world normally takes place through the agency of other people. The old view, he believes, tends to raise moral questions about God's wisdom and justice. If God were to intervene directly, it would (a) raise questions about the adequacy of His creation and (b), more importantly, raise questions about why God should intervene here and not there (for example, why should he not ward off a natural disaster, or an evil such as the Holocaust). This view is expressed by **Maurice Wiles**, in *God's Action in the World* (1986), when he says:

> *Miracles must by definition be relatively infrequent or else the whole idea of laws of nature ... would be undermined, and ordered life as we know it would be an impossibility. Yet even so it would seem strange that no miraculous intervention prevented Auschwitz or Hiroshima, while the purposes apparently forwarded by some of the miracles acclaimed in traditional Christian faith seem trivial by comparison.*

In the light of these changes in the theological understanding of miracles, the famous attack on miracles by **David Hume** appears somewhat beside the point. This is because Hume's attack was directed against the old understanding of miracles, which he understood as a 'transgression of the law of nature by a particular volition of the deity'. Since laws of nature are what people commonly observe happening, there could never be enough evidence to establish that a miracle happened.

On this strict empirical basis, Hume is of course correct. But, as we have seen, miracles need not be events of an extraordinary nature, since ordinary events can be seen as miracles. Hume was also reacting to the claim that miracles were crucial to religious faith, Christianity having been 'founded on miracle'. Here Hume was replying to the rationalism of **John Locke** (1632–1704), who had argued that Christian beliefs were solidly founded on prophecy and miracle. But the reality is that believers are much more flexible with regard to miracles than Hume or Locke realised.

*God and Experience*

Many Christians today, for instance, are prepared to discuss the possibility that the gospel miracles, which Hume took to be foundational to Christianity, may not have happened in the way they are described. Were this shown to be the case, Christianity would hardly collapse. **A. N. Wilson**, in his book *Jesus* (1980), argued that Jesus gained a large following because he was a gifted healer. If this was the case, his healings would have been natural events – but, to those who witnessed them, *seen as* miracles that showed the power of God.

Even the most special case – the event, or miracle, of the Resurrection – is open to a wide range of interpretations among theologians. These range from an understanding of the event as strictly historical (**Pannenberg**) to the view that it was a mysterious, but non-miraculous, *spiritual/religious* event within the understanding of the Apostles (**Bultmann**).

Many believers are also aware today of the philosophical problems of establishing the divine causality inherent in miracles. When the blind are said to see and the lame to walk, there is always the possibility of a natural explanation. A divine explanation is notoriously difficult to verify. However, as **Richard Swinburne** in *Faith and Reason* (1981) has pointed out, in the final analysis there is no contradiction in the idea of the author of nature suspending its laws for His own purposes. This is indeed the traditional understanding of miracle and one that, despite the problems it raises, can never be completely ruled out.

## Two views of miracles

**1 Direct intervention**
The traditional view. God intervenes directly to suspend the laws of nature. Examples from the life of Jesus. Most important example: the Resurrection

**2 Seeing as**
Events are 'seen as' signs of God's help, but may be explained as natural occurrences. Fits the traditional view of a miracle as event which causes wonder and evokes a religious response

*Why are miracles excluded by science? Which view of miracles is reconcilable with science?*

## II INTERPRETING EXPERIENCE: THEISM OR ATHEISM

As we saw in Chapter 1, all attempts to establish the existence of God by metaphysical reasoning (such as the Five Ways of Aquinas), were shown to be invalid by **Hume** and **Kant**. Our knowledge and ways of knowing are such that we cannot go beyond the world of our experience – the world of space and time – to posit the existence of a supernatural being called God (see Chapter 1).

But, as we saw, Kant in his moral argument went on to show that the idea of God can emerge from our awareness of duty. Kant thus changed the *locus* of the idea of God as a Being *outside* the world to a Being who could be found *within our experience*. This shift to personal experience as the place to find God was to dominate theology for at least the next century. As **James Richmond** in *Faith and Philosophy* (1966) said, 'It is apt to describe the nineteenth century as the century of religious experience'. The century would also be marked, as we shall see, by the start of a tradition in which an atheistic interpretation would be put on all claims of religious experience.

But we begin with the thinker who is generally regarded as the real founder of what can be called the theology of religious experience, **Friedrich Schleiermacher**.

## F. D. E. Schleiermacher (1768–1834)

Professor of theology at the University of Berlin, Schleiermacher came under the influence of **Kant** (1724–1804) and **Hegel** (1770–1831), and was a contemporary of both. His aim was to restore the credibility of religion among its 'cultured despisers'. From Kant, he took the idea that God could be found in personal experience of the world, but he disagreed with Kant that the place to look for God was in our moral experience. From Hegel, he took the idea that God had been made too transcendent, abstract and distant from the world, and that instead He should be thought of as immanent in the world, forming a unity with man.

These were ideas that had considerable biblical support. Man was made in God's 'image and likeness', and had been the vehicle of God's Incarnation in Jesus Christ, where the God–man unity reached its

*God and Experience*

Schleiermacher accepted the Enlightenment critique of metaphysics and tried to ground religion in experience. His influence has been immense

supreme form. For Schleiermacher, the link between God and man lay in man's capacity for intuitive awareness of contingency at the depths of his being. In his revolutionary book *On Religion: Speeches to its Cultured Despisers* (1799), he described how the awareness of God lay essentially within the feelings and emotions, especially the 'feeling of absolute dependence': '... religion consists in man's becoming conscious of his own limitations, of the fortuituous nature of his life as his being runs its course and silently disappears in the Infinite'. Paying heed to our inner feelings and intuitions would give us 'a sense and taste for the Infinite ... to drink in the beauty of the world ... to discover and love the Spirit pervading the cosmic whole'.

With ideas such as these, Schleiermacher would initiate a new approach to religion, and set a new trend in theological thinking, away from rational arguments and Church dogmas, towards *inner personal experience of God*. The danger was – as events would confirm – that a different conclusion could be drawn from Schleiermacher's experience of dependence within the boundless universe. Does this experience point to God as its origin and fulfilment, or is it an experience that really points to nothing more than the subjective awareness of our own human limitations? This question was asked and answered by our next thinker, Ludwig Feuerbach.

## Ludwig Feuerbach (1804–1872)

Brought up as a Christian, Feuerbach attended Hegel's lectures in Berlin. He became strongly influenced by the theological views of Hegel and Schleiermacher – but he believed that they were wrong. As **Karl Barth** put it, 'he tried to take [both] seriously ... in asserting the non-objective quality of God'.

Hegel's mistake was to claim that the Absolute (God) came to self-consciouness in man, and eventually became incarnate in man in Jesus Christ. Schleiermacher's mistake was to claim that we can intuit God's presence in our feelings and emotions. The truth is, as Feuerbach went on to argue in his highly influential *Essence of Christianity* (1841), that the whole idea of God is a *projection* on the part of man. Man is the ultimate reality. God is merely 'man writ large'. All the sublime attributes that we attribute to God should really be applied to our own nature: spirit, good will and perfect love all represent human aspirations, not divine qualities. God is the imaginary focus of all our human desires, drives, and longing for excellence and perfection.

Feuerbach believed that religion was still useful as long as man knew how to interpret it correctly. Beliefs such as the Resurrection represented man's aspiration to survive death and live forever. Prayer is useful to enable man to reflect on his own powers and capacities, and his needs. The significance of Jesus was that he was a supreme example of man's capacity for love and compassion towards his fellow man.

Thus did Feuerbach turn religion on its head, and, in the words of Karl Barth, turn *theology* (the science of God) into *anthropology* (the science of man). Feuerbach believed, as would many after him, that religion as traditionally understood was a hindrance to man's proper development in the world. By showing that religion was a projection of man's nature and powers on to an imaginary 'God', he hoped to liberate man from religious beliefs in another world, so that he would be freed to realise his true potentialities in this world.

(By way of ironic note, Feuerbach encountered serious opposition to his anti-religious ideas, which threatened his career as a philosopher. But by a fortuituous marriage he was able to retire to a German castle to pursue his speculative ideas about the fanciful nature of religious beliefs!)

## The influence of Feuerbach

Feuerbach's key idea, that God was only an imaginary projection of man's powers on to a supernatural being who had no real existence, was taken up and developed by later thinkers to form the basis of modern atheism. Two thinkers in particular stand out for the impact that they have had on the modern understanding of religion. They both produced theories that attempted to show that religion was a human invention as Feuerbach had claimed, and that it was something that humanity would be better off without. We begin with a brief look at the first of these thinkers, Feuerbach's contemporary Karl Marx.

*Karl Marx (1818–1883)*
Accepting Feuerbach's critique of religion as a projection, Marx put forward the theory that human ideas and beliefs are determined by peoples' material needs. 'Life is not determined by consciousness, but consciousness by life.' From this starting point, Marx went on to suggest that religious beliefs were a product of the human struggle for survival in society. The experience of social oppression and alienation gives rise to the need for comfort and consolation. The result is religious belief in a God who will reward people in another life as a substitute for the lack of material rewards in this.

Religion thus becomes '... the sigh of the oppressed creature, the heart of a heartless world, the soul of a soulless environment. It is the opium of the people.' Religion is then an expression of social distress, a turning to another world for comfort and consolation, and thus becomes a distraction from the real task of fighting against the causes of distress, poverty and injustice here and now. When the forces of alienation and oppression are defeated, and justice is restored, religion will no longer be necessary and will eventually wither away.

## Assessment of Marx

A full assessment of Marx's complex thought would be beyond the scope of this brief study. Suffice it to say that Marx's estimate of the role that religion has played in history, and his own experience of religion, played a major part in the conclusions that he reached. The rather negative role played by the Church of his day in regard to social reform, it has to be said, did little to make him think of religion as anything but the enemy of progress. An over-emphasis on other-worldly perspectives and values, at the expense of social involvement in the affairs of this world, confirmed for him that religion was an obstacle to social progress.

However, Marx may have failed to take into account that religion can be seen as an *effect* as well as a *cause*. What he certainly misjudged, and should have learned from history, was the hold that religion has on human beings. Particular forms of religion may have some roots in oppression and poverty. But religion, as history has shown, has other roots as well, and does not wither away when social circumstances of poverty and deprivation are removed.

In any case, it is hardly surprising that people should turn to religion for comfort when their material circumstances offer little else to hope for. **Malcolm Muggeridge**, then an atheist, while working as a journalist in Marxist Russia in the 1930s, provides a powerful and moving example in his book *The Green Stick* (1972):

> *In Kiev, where I found myself on a Sunday morning, on an impulse I turned into a church. It was packed tight ... young and old, peasants and townspeople, parents and children, even a few in uniform – it was a variegated assembly. The bearded priests, swinging their incense, intoning their prayers, seemed very remote and far away. Never before or since have I participated in such worship; the sense conveyed of turning to God in great affliction was overpowering. Though I could not, of course, follow the service, I knew from Klavdia Lvovna little bits of it; for instance where the congregation say there is no help for them save from God. What intense feeling they put into these words! In their minds, I knew, as in mine, was a picture of those desolate abandoned villages, of the hunger and the hopelessness, of the cattle trucks being loaded with humans in the dawn light. Where were they to turn to for help? Not to the Kremlin, and the Dictatorship of the Protelariat, certainly; nor to the forces of progress and democracy and enlightenment in the West ...*

## God and Experience

*Every possible human agency was found wanting. So, only God remained, and to God they turned with a passion, a dedication, a humility, impossible to convey. They took me with them; I felt closer to God then than I ever had before, or am likely to again.*

We can see from this example that religion can be a powerful source of strength and consolation to people in times of difficulty. Marx clearly found the conclusion irresistible that religion is the refuge of the desperate. Even more, it is an illusory refuge that distracts people from solving the problems of the here and now. History, he believed, confirmed this view. The biblical tradition of social criticism exemplified by the prophets, he argued, was largely relegated to a fringe aspect of the Christian faith.

The Church down the ages had tended to side with – and even prop up – whatever status quo regimes were in power, even when they were corrupt and oppressive. (Marx might find some confirmation of this in the reluctance of the official Church to offer much support to modern social justice movements, such as the admirable Liberation Theology.)

However, Marx's main failing had to be that of not making the distinction between the failures or abuses of religion and its supernatural truth claims. Marx found it easy to conclude that religion was discredited on the evidence of its apparent social inertia. This tendency of drawing conclusions about religion on the basis of human phenomena will also be apparent in the thought of our next highly influential figure, Sigmund Freud.

### Sigmund Freud (1856–1939)

Like Marx, Freud also accepted the Feuerbach critique of religion as a projection. But he offered his own unique interpretation of how the projection arises in the human mind. For Freud, the mechanism by which religion becomes an attraction to human beings is the way it appears as a solution to some fundamental human psychological needs.

These needs are first felt within the experiences of childhood. Freud uses the concept of childhood in a two-pronged way. He uses it in reference to the childhood of the individual, and in relation to what he called 'the childhood of the human race'. We begin with the latter. For this theory,

Freud borrows certain anthropological and historical assumptions which have been largely abandoned today.

In *Totem and Taboo* (1913), Freud argued that religion came from primitive man as a result of his earliest tribal experiences. Each tribe was ruled by a despotic male, who had control of all the women. This made him both loved for his protection, but hated for his power and control. Great tensions and jealousies were created among the other males, leading in the end to the despot being killed. The resulting sense of guilt and shame felt by the tribal males after the terrible deed is the essence of the so-called *Oedipus Complex* (named after the story of Oedipus, in Greek mythology, who killed his father to mate with his mother).

For Freud, this primal sense of guilt is the origin of all religion, and the key to its nature as a system that revolves round the appeasement of a heavenly father figure in order to obtain forgiveness. The original form of appeasement was twofold. It led, first, to the avoidance of the women of one's own tribe (taboo) and, secondly, to the killing and eating of the totem animal (totemism) as a ritual re-enactment of the patricidal deed.

These primitive tribal conflicts and tensions continue to be experienced within the human family in each succeeding generation. The father figure continues to occupy a position in which he is seen as both the source of protection (which is welcomed), and a source of law and restriction (unwelcomed). The father thus becomes the focus of two basic human needs: the need for protection from danger and the need for forgiveness. In this way, concluded Freud, the idea of God arises as a great cosmic father figure who can satisfy mankind's 'childish' needs.

Freud believed that his theory of religion as a 'universal obsessional neurosis' was confirmed by Christianity's emphasis on ritual sacrificial meals to appease the almighty to obtain forgiveness, and on its stress on future bliss in the life to come. For Freud, the conclusion was unmistakable. Religion is the product of wishful thinking, an illusion. In his *The Future of an Illusion* (1927), he described religious beliefs as 'not precipitates of experiences or end results of our thinking', but 'illusions, fulfilments of the oldest, strongest and most urgent wishes of mankind'.

## God and Experience

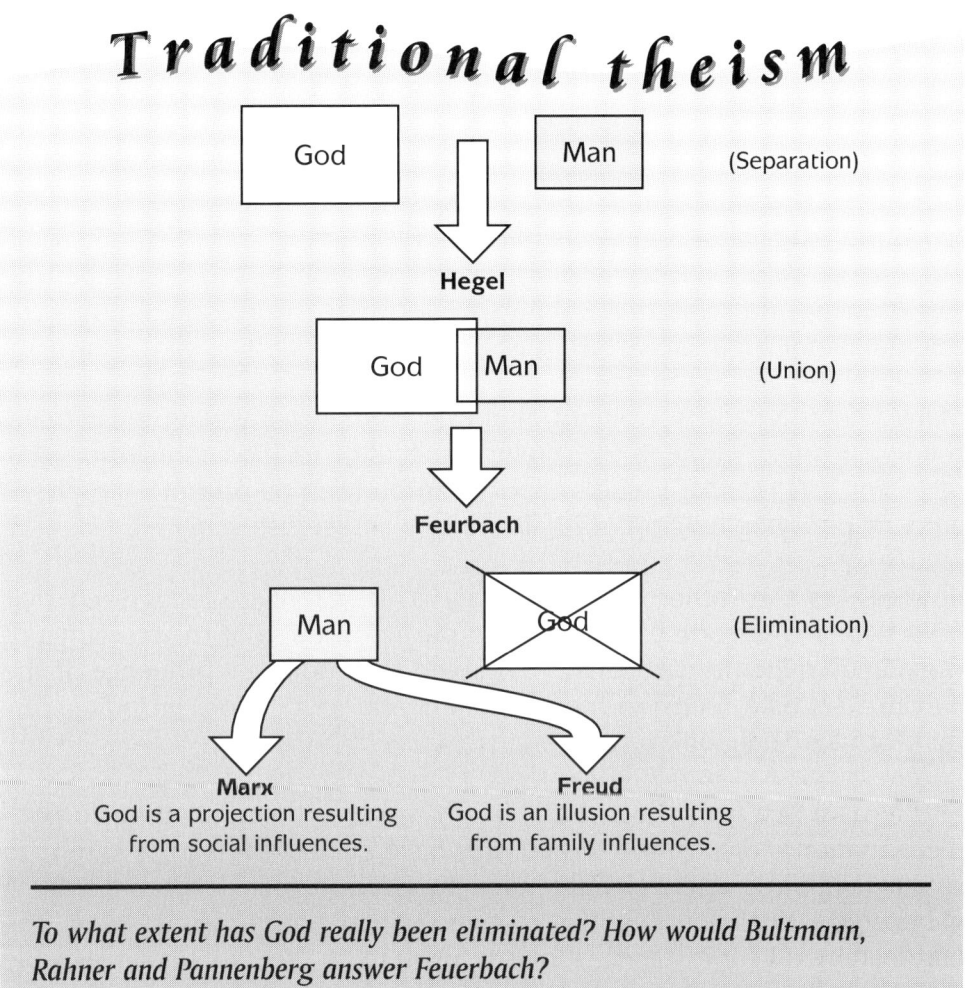

*To what extent has God really been eliminated? How would Bultmann, Rahner and Pannenberg answer Feuerbach?*

### Assessment of Freud

Limitations of space prevent us from giving a full assessment – or, indeed, a full account – of Freud's critique of religion. We can, however, highlight a number of important points.

First, Freud was convinced from the beginning that, as Feuerbach had held, religion was false. He also saw it as a diversion from the real task of solving the problems of the world, which only science was able to achieve.

Secondly, Freud was highly influenced by Darwin's theory of evolution.

Freud clearly absorbed this into his theory of religion, which he saw as an 'immature' and 'childish' phase of human development, something people would grow out of.

Thirdly, in spite of all this, Freud never went so far as to say that religion was *false*. He called it an *illusion*, not a delusion. An illusion can turn out to be the truth (for example, a mirage in the desert may turn out to be an oasis). A delusion is something at odds with reality and cannot be true (for example, if I think that I am Napoleon). For this reason, Freud's critique may not be as devastating as it first appears.

Many people would see Freud as no more than paralleling what many theologians have done in identifying aspects of religion as *myth* or *idolatry*. For this reason, Freud's theory can be seen as offering the possibility of purifying religion of its illusionary and selfish aspects.

Fourthly, as the father of psychoanalysis, it has to be recognised that Freud made a historic contribution to our knowledge of the workings of the human mind. In particular, he showed the important influence of the *unconscious* as a factor in human beliefs and motivation, including certain forms of religion.

Fifthly, as a result of the occupational hazard of being exposed to people of neurotic disposition, Freud may have overestimated the extent to which religion is really characterised by childish fears and concerns. A wider look at religion might have given him a more balanced view. The Old Testament, for instance, shows religion to be often an uncomfortable intrusion coming from outside the individual, rather than wish fulfilment from within, as Freud had believed (examples can be seen in Moses, Jonah, Job and Isaiah).

Sixthly, the idea of wish fulfilment is not exactly foreign to Christianity. An important aspect of the Christian faith is the virtue of *hope* that God will be true to His promise of salvation. But hope is never seen in isolation. As one of the three theological virtues, it must be accompanied by faith and *charity* (see 1 Cor. 13). Freud could therefore be criticised for highlighting the aspect of hope (wish fulfilment) at the expense of the other virtues, and making it look as if hope was the essence of religious belief.

Lastly, however, it has to be admitted that the influence of Freud's critique of religion has been far-reaching. Modern atheism can never be discussed without some reference to Freud. But, as **John Bowker** argued in *The Sense of God* (1973), Freud's theory was like a ramshackle machine, put together from odd bits he found lying around in the attic, but was never capable of flying. One of the most remarkable things about Freud's theory, he said, is not that it could be right but that it could never be proved wrong.

## *Carl Gustav Jung (1875–1961)*

An account of Freud's theory of religion would be somewhat incomplete without some reference to his eminent companion in the field of clinical psychology, C. G. Jung. At first, Jung shared Freud's critique that religion

Jung's assessment of religion was positive and sympathetic, unlike Freud's

was a projection from the unconscious, but he stopped well short of Freud by avoiding any judgements about whether it was true or false. As a result, Jung is seen to be much more sympathetic towards religion. This is partly because in his clinical experience he found that religion played a significant part in the integration of the individual towards mental health. He saw Freud's dismissal of religion as a direct product of nineteenth-century scientific atheism which, he believed, had been responsible for misunderstanding the whole nature of the human psyche.

Jung strongly disagreed with Freud's attempt to explain the working of the psyche in terms of *drives*, such as the sexual drive. This was a misplaced and inappropriate scientific explanation of something essentially *human*. Instead, Jung introduced the notion of the 'collective unconscious', a store of images (archetypes) common to all people, which enable them to interpret their experiences. Religion was an important factor in the life of the psyche, because it provided images that helped the individual to find personal spiritual integrity and inner peace.

Religion was thus an important source of the wisdom essential for mental well-being. He believed therefore, like James, that religion was important for its psychological benefits. In *Psychology and Religion: West and East* (1958), Jung showed the influence of **Otto**. He wrote:

> The term 'religion' designates the attitude peculiar to a consciousness which has been changed by the experience of the numinous.

For Jung, religion was essentially an attitude to life which is formed by the impact of a personal *experience* that transforms the psyche. The integration of the self, 'the goal of the mental life' is closely bound up with a religious belief. 'Among all my patients,' he said, '... there has not been one whose problem in the last resort was not that of finding a religious outlook on life'. This, we may note, is in sharp contrast with Freud, who saw religion as something that held up the individual's progress to mental adjustment. Significantly, though, Freud often conceded that religion could help people, but (never to be proved wrong) classed it as a 'crooked cure'!

## Simplifying the issue

**Atheism**
God does not exist. Therefore claims for religious experience must be explained in terms of human experience, traceable to human needs

**Theism**
God exists. Therefore it is perfectly conceivable that He can make Himself an object of religious experience

*How does this demonstrate the influence of* a priori *world views?*

### Friedrich Nietzsche (1844–1900)

We continue this section on the influence of Feuerbach with a brief look at another thinker whose ideas on God and religion would have far-reaching significance, both in the field of atheism and – for the reaction he provoked – also in the field of Christian theology. Friedrich Nietzsche was a brilliant theological student in his native Germany, but later became professor of classical philology at Basle University. He retired due to ill-health in 1879, and spent the rest of his life in solitude, ending in insanity. He is remembered for his aggressive attack on religious beliefs and practices.

He believed that religion created a slave mentality, elevated the weak and debilitated the strong. He believed that religious values should be replaced with values which energised the individual's 'will to power'. This will to power, when fully unleashed, and freed from the restraints of religion and culture, would produce the 'superman' and save the human race from decline. Nietzsche's morality is therefore 'nihilistic', standing for no particular or established set of values.

It is also openly atheistic. Nietzsche is especially remembered for his use of a term borrowed and reinterpreted from Hegel, 'the death of God'. For Nietzsche, God was dead as a matter of fact: people no longer believed in Him. God was also dead as a credible idea. The only viable alternatives therefore are nihilism and atheism.

Nietzsche's ideas were also to produce *secularism*, an attitude to the world (Latin *saecula*) that was distinctly non-religious. This would be fuelled by the growing acceptance of science as the provider of practical knowledge about life and the solver of its problems.

Nietzsche's contribution was taken seriously by later theologians, because they believed that much of what he said was true. Theism needed to be made more credible if the 'God is dead' catchphrase of modern atheism was to be proved wrong. This inspired **Paul Tillich** (among others) to create a theology that would answer Neitzsche, whose writings he had read. God is 'the ground of our being' who gives us 'the courage to be' and achieve our highest potential, not some transcendent being whose existence puts a brake on man's personal and social development.

In this way, Tillich hoped to construct a new concept of God that would help to counter the atheistic objections against the theism of his day (see Chapter 4).

### Emile Durkheim (1858–1917)

We conclude this section with a brief look at another thinker of considerable influence who reflected the ideas of Feuerbach, the French sociologist Emile Durkheim. Like Feuerbach, Durkheim saw religion in human and anthropological terms. In *The Elementary Forms of Religious Life* (1912), he gave a natural explanation of religion, describing it as a 'unified system of beliefs and practices relative to sacred things ... beliefs and practices which unite into one moral community called a Church, all those who adhere to them.'

Lying behind those words was Durkheim's naturalistic theory of religion as a product of the social group called 'society'. For Durkheim, 'God' is another name for the social group which was first represented in symbolic form by the totem ('at once the symbol of the god and of the society'). Far from being about a transcendent reality called God, religion is a function of man's awareness of himself as part of, and in relation to, society. The 'beliefs, myths, dogmas and legends' of religion are projections on to a supernatural being which arise from collective human experience.

Without going any further into his thought, because of lack of space, it is sufficient to notice how he has attempted, like his near contemporaries Marx and Freud, to put flesh on the bones of the religious critique of Feuerbach.

## Reductionist interpretations of religion

| | |
|---|---|
| A projection | Feuerbach |
| A sedative (opium) | Marx |
| An illusion | Freud |
| A deception | Nietzsche |
| A substitute | Durkheim |
| A focus of ideals | Cupitt |

*How devastating are these reductionisms?*

# III THE PROBLEM OF EVIL

We conclude this chapter on God and experience with a look at one of the great problems for Christian theism, again arising from an interpretation of human experience – what Hume called 'the rock of atheism', and has come to be called the problem of evil. Put briefly, the fact that there is so much apparently random evil and suffering in the world, coming from blind nature (natural evil) on the one hand, and human ill-will or wickedness (moral evil) on the other, makes the idea of an all-powerful and good God who cares for his creatures difficult to believe in.

The classical formulation of the problem was put forward as early as **Epicurus** (342–270 BC) and has since been repeated by **Augustine** and **Hume**. It is called the 'Inconsistent Triad' and is stated like this: 'Is God willing but not able to prevent evil? Then he is impotent. Is he able but not willing? Then he is malevolent. Is he both able and willing? Whence then is evil?' Put differently, if God is all powerful He can stop evil. If He is all loving, He will stop evil. But evil exists. Therefore ...?

The traditional Christian response to the fact of evil has not been to lose faith, but to put forward justifications for evil that would preserve the 'righteousness' of God. Such attempts are known as *theodicy* (from the Greek *theos*, God, and *dike*, just), a term first used by **Leibniz**. Its purpose is to demonstrate that, in spite of evil, God is just and righteous. Leibniz in fact believed that God created the best of all possible worlds *for the realisation of His purposes*. This idea seems to be central to most theodicies, and has been recently supported by **Peter Vardy** in *The Puzzle of Evil* (1992). We begin by considering the two traditional theodicies of **Irenaeus** and **Augustine**.

## *Views of evil*

**Atheistic**
The phenomenon of evil, whether natural or moral, is generally left for man to solve. There is no evidence to support the existence of a loving God of infinite power who cares for his creatures

**Theistic**
While it is not possible fully to understand evil, it is possible to reconcile its existence with a loving God. There must be a reason why God allows evil to happen. Part of the reason is that people choose to be evil, but in the end the victims of evil will be saved by God, whose love has been shown in the death of Christ

*How valid is the charge that the believer is not prepared to allow anything to count against the belief that God loves us? How is this answered?*

## The Augustinian theodicy

This was drawn up by **St Augustine** (354–430), and is based on an understanding of the Fall as described in Genesis 3. Borrowing St Paul's interpretation of the Fall in Rom. 5.12–20, Augustine argues that sin and death entered the world through the disobedience of our first parents. This brought about a disorder in our nature, and a disorder in creation. The fault was not God's, but man's. But it was a 'happy fault', because it caused the bringing about of so great a Redeemer, Christ. From the original disorder caused by man's sin, God brings about a new order made possible by the grace of Christ.

*The free will defence*
Closely allied to the Augustinian theodicy is the so-called *free will defence*. This is the view that evil is the result of man's misuse of his free will, beginning with Adam, and continuing ever since. In this view, evil is traceable to man, not to God. **Alvin Plantinga** has recently taken up a

further point made by Augustine, that the ultimate origin of evil can be traced to the misuse of free will by **Satan**, the leader of the bad angels, who rebelled against God in heaven. This act of disobedience and pride led to the infection of creation with all sorts of evil. If God wanted to prevent these evils, He would have to create human beings and angels without free will, and this He clearly did not wish to do. Instead, He tries to 'redeem' the situation by bringing good out of evil in His own mysterious way.

This has given rise to a debate about whether free will necessarily involved its misuse. Both **Anthony Flew** and **J. L. Mackie** have tried to argue that God could have created beings whose natures were such that they would always freely choose good. This raises the obvious question that if people are programmed always to choose good, how can they be genuinely free?

Both **John Hick** and **Richard Swinburne** strongly believe that evil and suffering are necessary elements of the world if people are to develop the higher virtues of courage, self-giving, love and compassion. While this line of argument belongs more properly with the **Irenaean** theodicy below, where its weaknesses will be discussed, it is necessary to mention it here. This is because it offers a second perspective on the *free will defence*. In this view, the genuine freedom to choose between good and evil is a requirement for the development of moral virtue, and therefore forms a justifiable *defence* of the existence of evil.

### Assessment of the free will defence

The main weakness of the free will defence is its failure to account for some important aspects of evil. It seems to ignore the following facts: (a) so much evil is often unjustifiably *caused to others* through one person's misuse of free will; (b) the misuse of free will by our first parents, and for that matter the 'bad angels', in the absence of a 'sinful nature', cannot easily be explained; and (c) if God is omniscient, He can hardly be excused responsibility from knowing the consequences of how His creatures would act.

**Huw Parri Owen**, in *Christian Theism* (1984), finds the free will defence unsatisfactory because of its theoretical nature, and because it leaves too many questions unanswered. He believes that, on its own, it is unable to offer much comfort to the people who are most involved in the problem of evil, those who suffer. We shall return to this idea below.

## The free will defence

| God gave man free will to be an essential part of his nature | Evil entered the world through sin, caused by man's misuse of his freedom, beginning with Adam | Without free will, man would be unable to make the moral choices necessary to test his character |
| --- | --- | --- |

*Assessment of Augustine's theodicy*

Augustine's theodicy appears to be noticeably impersonal. The emphasis is on justice, the restoring of a balance. Evil is seen as something which man deservedly brings on himself, and is therefore seen as essentially a punishment by God. It seems to leave a number of big questions unanswered. First, there is the question of the imbalance of evil; why some have to bear a larger share than others, for no apparent reason. Secondly, it fails to account for the origin of evil (through the serpent's temptation) at the beginning of man's life in the world. Thirdly, it ignores the historical fact that evil preceded man. If so, then the Fall is not a satisfactory explanation. Fourthly, the idea of man being perfect at the beginning of his history, and then falling from perfection, seems distinctly at odds with the facts of man's evolutionary history.

## The Irenaean theodicy

This theodicy, which is traceable to **St Irenaeus** (c.150 AD), has been revived in recent years by **John Hick** in his *Evil and the God of Love* (1966). In this theodicy, the world is the way it is to achieve God's plan and purpose; namely, to test man so that he develops the qualities necessary to be a noble soul. The world is therefore seen as 'a vale of soul-making', where physical and moral evil play their part in enabling man to grow into the sort of creature fit for His salvation. According to Irenaeus, man was first made in God's *image* (Gen. 1.26), but it was God's plan to make him grow into God's *likeness* (Gen. 1.26). For this to happen, man had to be tested. This life provides the ideal conditions for this to happen.

Man is given evil and suffering to enable him to develop the character qualities that will enoble him: courage, generosity, kindness and love. Part of the test is the 'epistemic' distance that evil creates between man and God. This means that man lives in a kind of fog which makes God's presence difficult to see, and hence makes faith more virtuous. The story of the Fall is a mythological account of man's testing. Its outcome made it necessary for Christ to come, in order to set an example that man could follow, and to show him how to find his true salvation with the help of grace.

### Assessment of Irenaeus's theodicy

This theodicy has the advantage that it accords better than the Augustinian account with the facts of evolution. It allows for the idea of growth and development in the achievement of moral virtue. On the other hand, it does not easily explain (a) why Adam and Eve failed even though they were not at an epistemic distance from God, and (b) why they were held fully responsible by God even though they were supposedly at an immature stage of moral development, and might therefore be 'excused' for their Fall.

Another problem with this theodicy is that it appears to suggest not only that 'suffering is good for you' but that without suffering great virtue cannot be achieved. This is often put forward to justify physical evil, such as earthquakes, famine, disease and so on. Such a view is taken by **Richard Swinburne** in *The Existence of God* (1979). He argues that the world needs to have evil in it for man to develop morally. This is to overlook three awkward facts: (1) that many people could claim to have lived virtuous lives without ever having suffered; (2) that many who have suffered have been embittered and even dehumanised by it; and (3) the view that suffering is good is difficult to square with Jesus' attitude to suffering. In the gospel we see Jesus trying to eliminate suffering, in fulfilment of one of the signs of the Messianic age (Luke 4.18f.).

Finally, we have to say that one of the real difficulties for the theist in justifying God is the seemingly senseless and random occurrence of evil: many people feel that there is no apparent reason to the way in which evil and suffering are distributed. Because of these difficulties, it would appear that neither of these theodicies on their own would have much practical value in helping a person to cope with evil.

Many believers, therefore, have tended to seek a solution within their own faith, in terms of the kind of theodicy reflected, for instance, in the New Testament. In this more 'religious' approach, which draws on the resources of the Christian faith, many of the objections raised above would be absorbed into the whole mystery of suffering.

## New Testament theodicy

It could be argued that the above theodicies are too *theoretical*, inasmuch as they offer rational accounts of why God must be right to allow evil. They offer, it could be said, cold comfort to believers who have to cope with the reality of evil in everyday life. This cannot be said of the theodicies put forward by **St Paul** and other writers in the New Testament. These theodicies, which are eschatological in nature, are based on God's future promises. Paul's approach is to contrast the present-world sufferings and misfortunes with the rewards and glory to come:

> *I consider that our present sufferings are not worth comparing with the glory that will be revealed in us.* (Rom. 8.18)
>
> *Who shall separate us from the love of Christ? Shall trouble or hardship or persecution or famine? ... No, in all these things we are more than conquerers through him who loved us ... I am convinced that neither death nor life ... will be able to separate us from the love of God in Christ Jesus Our Lord.* (Rom. 8.35f.)

**St Peter** writes: 'though now for a little while you may have to suffer grief in all kinds of trials. These have come so that your faith may be proved genuine ... (1 Pet. 1.6–7)

In **Revelation** there is the promise to those who suffer that 'Never again will they hunger, never again will they thirst ... and God will wipe away every tear from their eyes.' (Rev. 7.15f.)

From these passages it can be seen that the problem of evil is set in the context of God's future promises of glory and reward for those who remain faithful to Christ.

# Suffering and God's mercy

A case for saying that suffering is limited by God's mercy can be made by pointing to five aspects:

1 temporality (all suffering ends with death)

2 love of others (human comfort), given in suffering

3 inspiration of faith (source of courage) in time of distress

4 value (now and in the hereafter) – soul-making and salvation

5 alternative option (*Angst*, lack of meaning) – despair

---

*To what extent do those points give an answer to Flew (p. 145)? Do these aspects form part of theoretical or practical theodicy?*

## The choice: faith or atheism

Two sharply contrasting responses to the problem of evil may be summarised under the headings of faith and atheism. For some, the fact of evil and suffering is a denial of the existence of God. For others, it compels the rejection of a God whom they cannot exonerate for allowing some evils to happen. This latter response has been famously illustrated by **Fyodor Dostoyevsky**, in his novel *The Brothers Karamazov*. One of the brothers, Ivan, refuses to believe in a God who allows innocent children to suffer, and rejects the suggestion that such suffering can ever be justified, even on the grounds that innocent victims will be compensated in the hereafter.

A similar attitude is expressed by the unbelieving **Albert Camus**. In *The Plague* (1948), many die helplessly, including children. The priest says 'Perhaps we should love what we cannot understand.' The doctor replies: 'Until my dying day I shall refuse to love a scheme of things in which children are put to torture.'

## Questions about God

By contrast, others have managed to retained their faith even through the most harrowing experiences. **Elie Wiesel**, in *Night* (1958), describes such an experience in Auschwitz. 'The S.S. hung two Jewish men and a boy before the assembled inhabitants of the camp. The men died quickly but the death struggle of the boy lasted half an hour. "Where is God? Where is he?", a man behind me asked. And I heard a voice within me answer, "Here he is – he is hanging here on this gallows".' A somewhat similar response is reflected in the story of the three rabbis in Auschwitz. They put God on trial and found Him guilty of allowing the Holocaust to happen. When they had finished, one of them said 'it is the hour of prayer'. And they all bowed their heads in silence to pray.

The German theologian **Jurgen Moltmann**, in *The Crucified God* (1974), believes that the most fruitful theodicy is one that relies on the Christian belief in the death of Christ. In this perspective, hope is offered that God is not detached from or unaware of human suffering because 'God died on the cross of Christ'. (For more on the idea that God does not intervene, but suffers in the world, see also Chapter 4, Process theology.) At the same time, Moltmann believes that evil and suffering are not willed by God and should be fought against by all mankind. He believes that the constant presence of human hope for a better future is itself an insight into the reality of God's presence among men.

## *Theodicies*

| Theoretical | Practical |
|---|---|
| Evil is an inevitable part of reality and is permitted by God (a) for His own mysterious purposes, (b) as a consequence of man's sin and (c) to enable man to develop the moral qualities of a noble soul through trial and testing | The scriptures assure us that God rewards innocent suffering (St Paul). The Cross shows that God himself has suffered (Moltmann). God is man's companion and fellow sufferer (process theology) |

*In what sense do evil and suffering remain the greatest challenge to faith?*

## A summary of the problem

We may conclude this section on the problem of evil by summarising the main points. Evil and suffering can provide a basis for an atheistic interpretation of the world. They appear to undermine belief in a God who is omnipotent and all loving. They are also capable of casting doubt on the credibility of God for some believers.

At the same time, evil and suffering have not made faith in God impossible. Believers down the centuries have searched for ways to reconcile suffering with faith in a loving God. At the theoretical level, they have been offered help by the theodicies of Augustine and Irenaeus. Augustine's theodicy has helped to show that evil and suffering are somehow not part of the way God intended the world to be. The Irenaean theodicy has helped to show that evil and suffering are part of God's plan for His creatures to grow in virtue and goodness. Perhaps there is the possibility of a middle ground, with evil seen as not intended by God, but now used by Him to bring forth good.

At the practical level, evil has been seen as a mystery from which God has not been absent. This belief has been made possible by faith in the mystery of the Cross, in which God has been involved through the death of His Son. It has also been confirmed as a realistic hope by the assurance of the scriptures that the sufferings of this world, no matter how terrible they may be, cannot be compared to the glory to come. At the same time, evil remains a mystery that can never be fully understood. Perhaps in the end it is best seen as a paradox, something willed – and, at the same time, not willed – by God.

> HOW GOD BECOMES AN OBJECT
>
> *By its very nature the eternal You cannot become an It; because by its very nature it cannot be placed within measure and limit, not even within the measure of the immeasurable and the limit of the unlimited; because by its very nature it cannot be grasped as a sum of qualities, not even as an infinite sum of qualities that have been raised to transcendence; because it is not found either in or outside the world; because it cannot be experienced; because it cannot be*

*thought; because we transgress against it, against that which has being, if we say: 'I believe that he is' – even 'he' is still a metaphor, while 'you' is not.*

*And yet we reduce the eternal You ever again to an It, to something, turning God into a thing, in accordance with our nature. Not capriciously. The history of God as a thing, the way of the God-thing through religion and its marginal forms, through its illuminations and eclipses, the times when it heightened and when it destroyed life, the way from the living God and back to him again, the metamorphoses of the present, of embedment in forms, of objectification, of conceptualisation, dissolution and renewal are one way, are the way.*

Martin Buber

# Chapter 4 | God and Language

In this chapter, we shall look at the way in which religious language is used by believers as they try to express the beliefs of their faith. Secondly, we shall look at the challenge to the meaning of religious language presented by *logical positivism*. In response to this challenge, we shall see how the theological and philosophical problems of talking about God have been brought into sharper focus, leading some theologians to find some empirical point of intersection with the mystical nature of religious language. We shall then consider the question raised by Wittgenstein: Of what kind of experience is religious language an expression? We shall finally consider the attempts of theologians to get behind the use of words and look for a new way of *thinking* about God. This will be seen as an attempt to find a better way of *speaking* about God that is more intelligible to what is variously called 'modern man', 'secular man', 'scientific man' or, in the words of **Dietrich Bonhoeffer**, 'man come of age'.

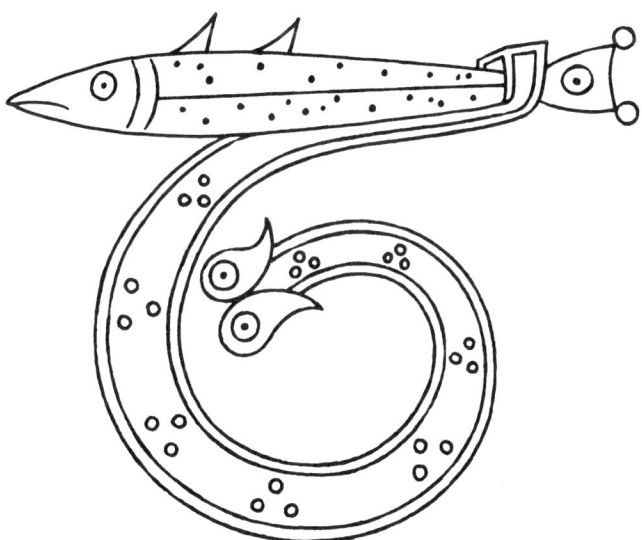

Illuminated letter 'T', Book of Kells, Ireland. Religious language has a long literary history. Here is a striking example of the sacred letter 'T' (Theos) from the eighth-century masterpiece

## Questions about God

We begin, however, with the way in which believers have traditionally spoken about God.

## I SPEAKING ABOUT GOD

We begin with the two fundamental ways of speaking about God, the *via affirmitiva*, and the *via negativa*. In the 'affirmative' way, positive things are said about God. He is said to be good, just, loving, infinite and so on. Many theologians say that the affirmative way must always be supplemented by the 'negative' way. Whatever we say about God must be qualified or corrected by 'taking back' or 'denying' what we have said. This is because we can only speak about God using language that we normally use about people and things in the world. This is the meaning of *analogy* (comparison). But because God is *infinitely* beyond us, we cannot hope to express truths about Him without constant qualification of our language. **Dionysius the Areopagite** gives some indication of the difficulty of speaking about God in a passage from his *Mystical Theology*:

> Once more, ascending yet higher, we maintain that It is not soul, or endowed with the faculty of imagination, conjecture, reason, or understanding; nor can It be described by the reason or perceived by the understanding, since It is not number, or order, or greatness, or equality, or inequality, and since It is not immovable nor in motion, nor at rest, and has no power, and is not power or light, and does not live, and is not life ... nor does It belong to the category of non-existence or to that of existence; nor do existent beings know It as It actually is ... nor can any affirmation or negation apply to It ...

In this rather torturous passage, Dionysius gives us a flavour of what it is like to speak about God. We can see how he takes the *via negativa* almost to the limit.

### The way of analogy

Believers, however, have always insisted that many things can be said about God using the *via affirmativa*, or *via positiva*, provided that it is qualified – qualified, that is, by recognising that language about God is nearly always by way of *analogy*. Thus when the believer says 'the Lord is my shepherd' or even 'God is loving', or when God is spoken of as a *person*, allowance is made for the fact that these words are not being applied to God in the way we would apply them to another human being.

## Religious metaphors

Father    King    Shepherd
   Judge    Rock    Fortress
  Shield    Light
       Bread    Water

**Thomas Aquinas** underlined the nature of analogy by saying that when we speak about God we use words and images neither *equivocally* and *univocally*. 'Univocally' means in the same sense as when we apply them to ourselves. So, for example, when we say God is wise or just, we do not understand these terms as applying exactly to God in the same sense as they apply to ourselves. 'Equivocally' means applying the same terms in a completely different sense. Because we are made in God's image and likeness, we can assume some similarity between ourselves and God. But we are neither exactly the same as God nor completely different from Him. Therefore we can legitimately speak about God using comparisons (analogies) with ourselves. Aquinas also distinguished between analogy of *attribution*, which involves attributing to God what applies to ourselves (things such as existence, goodness, beauty etc.), and analogy of *proportionality*, which means remembering that God is infinitely beyond human beings (see Ramsey's models and qualifiers below).

Others have said that the easiest way to speak of God is to remember that His attributes are infinitely greater and more perfect than ours. Religious believers are normally unaware that they are using analogies, but on reflection they would recognise that words and language about God have to be qualified to take into account the transcendent reality of their subject. They would also on reflection accept that language about God has to draw on the empirical world of human experience if it is to express anything about God.

The world of human experience provides the linguistic resources to

God creating the sun and the moon, Salisbury Cathedral, England, thirteenth century. Here God is depicted anthropologically and analogically as a person of supreme power

enable human beings to speak coherently about God without falling victim to naive realism. For instance, when God is said to be 'up there' it does not mean (as the Russian cosmonaut Yuri Gagarin thought) that God is somewhere up in the sky. The idea that God is in the heavens is an archetypal idea to express the fundamental truth of God's transcendence, as Wittgenstein astutely noted in the way people 'lift their eyes'.

**Joseph Runzo**, in *Is God Real?* (1993), argues that the empirical language which we use in everyday life acts as a bridge between ourselves and God. 'It is a matter of *faith* that one's theological conceptions ... and one's religious experiences ... do provide the basis for properly referring to, and therefore speaking about God ...'

But is it not also the case that some terms or attributes can be applied to God *literally*? In what other sense can we speak of the traditional attributes of God? When we say, for instance, that God is infinite, perfect, eternal, omnipotent, omniscient or transcendent, surely we are using language about God in its literal sense, while allowing for the fact that we have no way of knowing how exactly those terms apply to God.

In the ordinary course of events, however, religious language employs images, symbols, models, metaphors, similes and myth drawn from the natural world to express truths about God. As **Wittgenstein** said in his typically enigmatic way, the mystical cannot be expressed, *but it can be contained* in the empirical. In the following section, we shall look at the use of symbols and the nature of religious language as symbolic.

## Symbolic language

Once we move away from describing the attributes of God which, we have argued, involves using language about God literally, we then enter the realm of using language about God *symbolically*. The use of analogy is one aspect of this. Thus to say that 'God is my protector and shield', or 'The Lord is my rock and my fortress', is to employ the image or metaphor of a shield, rock or fortress, images taken from the world of experience as symbols for God. **Ian Ramsey**, in *Religious Language* (1965), uses the idea of *models*. A model is an image or a concept taken from everyday experience which can be used to throw light on the reality of God. Models can be abstract, such as wisdom, power or goodness; or personal, such as king, shepherd or father. However, when models are applied to God they need to be suitably *qualified*; for example, God is *infinitely* wise and *all* powerful. He is a *mighty* king or an *almighty* father. Accompanied by the qualifier, the model then lights up the nature of God and hopefully evokes a suitable disclosure leading to a commitment, says

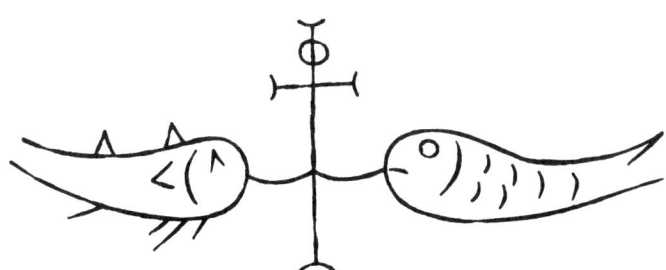

The Christian fish symbol on a grave in the catacomb of Domitilla, Rome, from the third century. The fish was a symbol of both Christ and the Christian soul. The anchor was a symbol of hope (Heb. 6.19), made possible by the Cross. Can these symbols be called meaningless? How can their meaning be defended using Wittgenstein's 'forms of life' theory (see p. 153)? Why is this explanation unsatisfactory for believers?

Ramsey. In practice, a multiplicity of models is needed to do justice to the reality of God.

## Religious language

Myths  Art  Images  Symbols
Analogies
Similes  Metaphors
Models  Architecture  Parables

**John Macquarrie**, in *God Talk* (1967), thinks that the most suitable language to use in speaking about God should be the language of *existence*. By this, he means talking about God as the source of our existence, the power that 'opens up' our capacity to truly exist. He proposes that the traditional symbol of *light* as a symbol of God should be replaced by 'openness', the characteristic quality of being which lets everything 'be'. Many will not find this as helpful as Macquarrie thinks. The mysterious quality of light, the fact that we do not see light but only *by means of* light, its widespread location, its power to give or support life and its non-physical, almost spiritual, nature makes it hard to improve on as a helpful symbol of the nature of God for many believers.

In speaking about the language of religion, it would be a serious omission to leave out the fields of art and architecture as bearers of truths about God. Art conveys a sense of the holy through the symbolism of human beings who embody the divine through faith, goodness and holiness; and through the depiction of historical events of religious significance. The great masters of the Renaissance provide numerous examples. In the field of architecture, one has only to think of the great cathedrals, such as Chartres, Canterbury or Burgos (to name but a few). These stunning structures have a special power to convey a sense of the numinous, both in the daring of their architecture and the splendour of their iconography. By themselves, projecting from their surroundings and pointing heavenwards, they stand as historic symbols of what the divine meant to the people who built them (see p. 142).

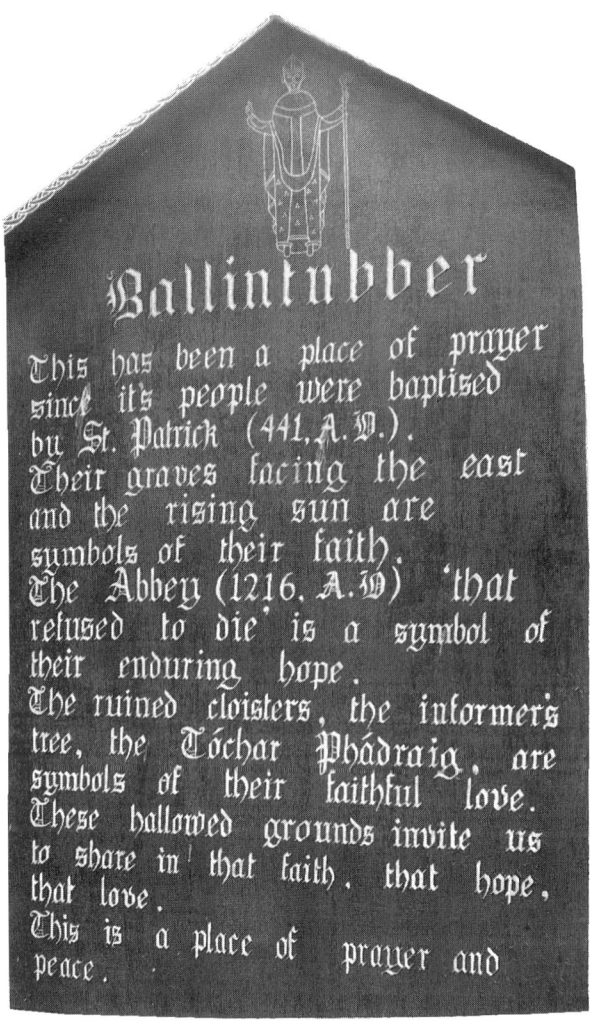

An interesting example of religious symbolism in an ancient Irish abbey

## Myth

We continue this section on how believers use religious language to speak about God with a brief consideration of the language of myth. In its broad sense, myth is an attempt to explain aspects about the world and its origins in *story* form. The story of creation in Genesis is often referred to as the creation *myth*. Unfortunately, in popular usage the word 'myth' is used to refer to stories that are fictional, and hence it has come to have a pejorative overtone. **Rudolf Bultmann** (see below)

## Questions about God

Religious language in stone (in this case, York Minster, England). In what way – or ways – does the cathedral speak the language of faith?

defined myth as any story in which God is seen to act like another human being. The effect of this is to make people lose sight of the *meaning* of the story, and dismiss the whole thing as naive and unbelievable. So, to take the creation myth: the real meaning of this story is that God is the creator, and man stands before God in a fallen state of creaturely dependence. Bultmann has been criticised for paying too little attention to the analogical nature of Bible stories about God, and for creating the impression that all such stories are merely vehicles of meaning. Those who have reacted to Bultmann have wanted to insist that many of the biblical stories are truly *historical events* (such as the Resurrection of Christ) and that their meaning depends on their historical claim to be events that happened. In other words, to overlook the historical validity of many of the biblical narratives is precisely to undermine their meaning.

## Justifying religious language

The problem, however, for religious believers is to justify their talk about God to outsiders, and to show that in religious language they are referring to something real when they speak about God. They need to show that language involving symbols, images and metaphors applies to something beyond the empirical world. The need to explain the meaning of religious language, and what such language means when used to talk about a transcendent reality called God, has been brought into very sharp focus in recent years by the challenge of *logical positivism*. This was a movement that took as its starting point that only empirical truths and statements about empirical realities deserve to be called meaningful. On the other side of the coin, so-called transcendent or metaphysical truth claims were declared meaningless. Since the early days of its emergence, it has been notorious in criticising the alleged vagueness of the language of religion, compared with the alleged clarity and distinctness of the language of science. To this criticism we now turn.

## II THE CHALLENGE OF LOGICAL POSITIVISM

Logical positivism is a philosophical movement that began in the 1920s, for the purpose of studying and analysing the use of language. One of its presuppositions is that 'language mirrors the world'. The task of philosophy is therefore to check and clarify the use and meaning of language, especially language about the world. 'The world', in the words of the father figure of logical positivism, **Ludwig Wittgenstein**, 'is everything that is the case'. What is the case, unfortunately for theology, was everything that can be proved and verified by observation and experience. As its name suggests, the new movement was an offshoot of *positivism* (what can be 'posited' or proved). Positivism was a nineteenth-century movement associated with the French thinker **Auguste Comte** (1798–1857). It assumed that the only genuine knowledge is that which is obtained by the methods of science. All other claims to knowledge, such as metaphysical speculation or religion, should be abandoned. In fact, Comte believed that human history followed three phases, each representing a different stage of progress in human development: the theological, the metaphysical and the positive. Only the last phase should be taken seriously. We can detect here echoes of the *empiricism* of **Hume**, and a confident assumption of the superiority of the methods of empirical science in the quest for knowledge and truth.

There was also the hidden assumption that religion was a system of belief which depended for its credibility on its capacity to offer causal explanations for things in the world. With this assumption, it would not be surprising that religion would be regarded with prejudice. Compared to science, its outlook would be regarded as naive, its claims to know truths about reality unverifiable, and its language meaningless.

Logical positivism could rightly be called the 'linguistic wing' of positivism. Its function would be to act as watchdog over the way in which language was used, and to adjudicate over its meaning. It would not be difficult to predict that, in its view, the language of science would have a special pre-eminence.

Logical positivism began to take shape when a group of philosophers came together in Vienna in 1927 to discuss the ideas contained in Wittgenstein's *Tractatus* (1921). They called themselves the Vienna Circle. They believed that since all knowledge about the world is based on experience, this fact should also determine what is to count as *meaningful* and *meaningless* in language. Thus was coined the *verification principle*.

## Verification principle

Only statements that are analytical or empirically verifiable are meaningful. Statements of theology and metaphysics are meaningless

*How have theologians responded to this claim?*

## Verification and falsification

In simple language, a statement which cannot be verified by some form of sense experience is meaningless. Statements about the world were called *synthetic* statements because they bring together (synthesise) factual nouns and predicates to produce *cognitive* (knowledge-filled) propositions – for example, 'my coat is wet'. *Analytical* statements (or tautologies) were taken for granted as meaningful (but trivial) because they are circular. This makes them *non-cognitive*. 'Non-cognitive' means that they give us no new information about reality. For example, to say 'a husband is a married man' or 'A straight line is the shortest distance between two points' is simply to spell out or analyse the meaning of a certain word or term.

Measured against the verification principle, statements of metaphysics (about things that lie behind the world of experience) and religion (about God and the supernatural) were classed as *nonsensical* or *meaningless*. This was because (a) they could not be verified and (b) they made no difference to how the world is since they are consistent with all possible states of affairs (see Flew below). It is not difficult to see that the challenge to religious language posed by logical positivism was a new extension of the challenge posed by science. Both were based on the claim that the only kind of truth worthy of the name is that which can be obtained and verified by sense experience.

**A. J. Ayer**, in *Language, Truth and Logic* (1936), helped to spread the new linguistic philosophy to England. Ayer introduced two important distinctions to do with verification. The first was the distinction between verification in theory and in practice. Even if something could not be verified in practice, such as a scientific law (for example, 'all metals expand when heated') or a general assumption (such as 'all leopards have spots'), such statements are still meaningful, it is claimed, because we know what sense experience would count towards verifying them.

Another distinction was that between 'weak' and 'strong' verification. Some things, such as atoms, cannot be observed directly, but certain other observations can help to verify statements about them. This led to the definition that 'the meaning of a statement is the method of its verification'.

Yet despite these distinctions, religious statements (for example, 'God exists', 'God loves us', 'God is three persons in one nature', 'Jesus sits on the right-hand of God', etc.) remain meaningless, say the positivists, because there is no method for their verification. Later, **Anthony Flew** introduced the 'principle of falsification'. In science, a theory is often held to be a working hypothesis as long as it is not falsified. Flew held that if a statement or belief cannot be falsified – that is, if nothing is allowed to count against it – it is meaningless. To illustrate how religious beliefs (and the language used to express them) cannot be falsified, Flew made use of a *parable*.

The parable is about two explorers who come upon a clearing in the jungle. In the clearing, many flowers and many weeds are growing. One is convinced that a gardener comes and tends the flowers, while the other disagrees, pointing to the weeds as evidence that no gardener comes. For Flew, this is exactly how the believer holds on to beliefs for which there is no empirical evidence. And although the weeds seem to disprove the existence of a gardener, nothing shakes the believer's conviction that a gardener exists. Flew's conclusion is that any belief or statement of belief is meaningless if it cannot be falsified by any evidence against it. Flew takes the example of the belief that 'God loves us'. He maintains that no conceivable state of affairs (for example, evil and suffering) is allowed to falsify this belief, since the believer will always insist that 'God knows best', or 'God still loves us'.

In reply to Flew, the believer might want to say three things. First, it is a natural part of faith to trust in God. This is not irrational trust, because the believer is happy to believe that God has made known His love in other ways (for example, from the Incarnation and death of Christ). Secondly, on balance there are sufficient empirical grounds in the experience of life to support faith in God's love. A world of unrelieved evil and malice is logically conceivable. If such a world existed, Flew might have a stronger case. But such a world, most people would agree, does not exist.

This view is supported by **Robert Prevost** in *Probability and Theistic Explanation* (1990). Since religious beliefs are based on trust, this trust should hold no matter what temptations confront the believer. While Prevost allows for the possibility that this trust could be undermined, he argues that it is rational to believe that it will not be, and that time will vindicate it. To use a metaphor in reply to Flew, there is enough depth of happiness, goodness and hope in the sea of life to enable the ship of faith to float.

Thirdly, to take the analogy of parental love, when we are disciplined or punished by our parents it does not logically lead us to doubt that they still love us. Why should it be different with a believer's relationship to God, a relationship based on trust?

We shall return to the question of verification again in the following section, when we look at how theologians have responded to the logical positivist challenge.

## Responses to logical positivism

The attack on religious language by Anthony Flew provoked a vigorous debate among a number of philosophers and theologians. All attempted in some way to show that Flew's criticism was not conclusive. They tried to show that the language of religion, while not verified by experience, is not falsified by experience either. This partly explains something that Flew appears to have overlooked; namely, why believers hold on to their beliefs at all, and do not consider it irrational to do so.

**John Wisdom** makes exactly this point in his original parable about a garden (from which Flew's more slanted parable is adapted). Wisdom's original parable was used to show how believers look to patterns in the world that support their beliefs. The parable is about two people who return to their long-neglected garden and find, among the weeds, that a few of the old plants are surprisingly vigorous. One says to the other, 'It must be that a gardener has been coming and doing something about these weeds.' The other disagrees and an argument ensues, following the same pattern as in Flew's parable above. But there is a significant difference between the parables. Wisdom's parable has much more realistic evidence of a possible gardener (orderly plants in a neglected garden). By comparison, Flew's version is more far-fetched and unrealistic (flowers and weeds in a jungle clearing). Wisdom's parable is closer to illustrating religious beliefs and language than Flew's, because it illustrates beliefs that are realistic and reasonably well-founded. As **James Richmond** points out in *Theology and Metaphysics* (1970), the original purpose of Wisdom's parable was to show that religion is something consistent with empirical facts about the world. Religion is not an outlook which has no regard for the facts. In Wisdom's parable, the existence of vigorous plants (aspects of the world) supports belief in a gardener (God).

The main point, however, is that the believer's faith is founded on aspects of the world that are seen to support that faith. This means that statements of belief are what believers claim they are – legitimate interpretations of reality consistent with patterns perceived in the world. As Wisdom says, the existence of God is not an *experimental* issue that it is possible to decide one way or the other. He compares it to the way we make judgements about things such as beauty: 'The difference as to whether a God exists ... is like a difference as to whether there is beauty in a thing.' Flew's falsification principle, therefore, is not as devastating as it might first appear. As **Basil Mitchell** points out, religious beliefs are not amenable to falsification, but they are still a legitimate interpretation of reality based on observable data from the empirical world.

Another insight into the nature of religious language has been provided by the philosopher **R. M. Hare**. He agreed with Flew that religious language was non-cognitive because it couldn't be falsified, but disagreed that it was meaningless. In fact, we all have beliefs that we insist on holding in spite of evidence that might undermine them. Hare called these beliefs *bliks*. He showed how bliks work in a parable about a certain lunatic, who is convinced that all dons are out to murder him. The student remains convinced even when dons are nice to him. When this happens, he thinks that the dons are being devious and hypocritical, showing the need to be on his guard. Hare's blik theory illustrates the unshakeable nature of religious beliefs, but as an account of the nature of religious faith it is not very flattering.

Most believers are convinced that they have very good reasons to hold on to their beliefs – unlike the lunatic, who appears to have no grounds at all for believing that all dons are out to murder him. However, the main point of the blik theory is that a blik is meaningful even if it cannot be falsified, because it affects a person's *attitude*, or the way he or she feels about something.

A much more true to life parable has been used by Basil Mitchell to illustrate how religious beliefs are held on *trust*. He argues that religious assertions and beliefs are meaningful, because – although not falsifiable in practice – they are falsifiable in principle. This seems to mean that they are at least provisionally cognitive. Mitchell's parable goes like this. In an occupied country during a war, a resistance fighter meets a mysterious stranger and spends a night in earnest conversation. The stranger tells the fighter to trust that he is on the side of the resistance, even if at times he might be seen helping the enemy. The parable goes on to show how the fighter's faith in the stranger is constantly tested. Despite being tempted to lose faith in the stranger, as he sometimes sees him appearing to help the enemy and sometimes not, the fighter always says to himself 'The stranger knows best.' Mitchell says it is impossible to tell at what point the fighter might lose faith in the stranger. In this way, the parable is a good illustration of how a believer's faith works. As Mitchell says, many things count against religious faith, but so also do many things help to keep it alive. As a result, the believer continues to trust

God because nothing in experience counts *decisively* to undermine this trust. Thus, for Mitchell, religious beliefs are open to empirical falsification in principle and are therefore meaningful, even if in practice it is impossible to say what would falsify them.

Another philosopher who has tried to show that religious language is meaningful is **John Hick**. He appeals to what is called *eschatological verification* (*eschaton* is Greek for 'the after-life'). Like Mitchell, he believes that religious people hold their beliefs on trust. Religious beliefs are accepted as credible now, but will one day be proved to be true. Hick too has a parable to illustrate this. It is taken from **John Bunyan's** *Pilgrim's Progress* and is about two people on a journey. One is convinced that it leads to the Celestial City, while the other believes that it leads nowhere; but since this is the only road there is, both must travel it. Both have similar experiences on the road, but each interprets them differently from the other. One lives in expectation of the final destination, while the other has no such expectation. One sees the adventures on the journey as either trials and comforts sent by God, while the other simply sees them as either good fortune or bad. Only when they reach the end of the road will the truth be known. Hick's theory, of course, begs the question as to how it could be verified that there are grounds for believing in a celestial city (an after-life). Nevertheless, the idea of trusting in what the future holds is not logically irrational, and is indeed quite common. In fact, Hick's theory has the merit of being a reasonable account of how religious language is taken on trust: the ordinary believer is prepared to wait for verification of his beliefs in God's good time, for that is the nature of faith.

## The parables

The Overgrown Garden (Wisdom)
The Jungle Clearing (Flew)
The Paranoid Student (Hare)
The Resistance Worker (Mitchell)
The Celestial City (Hick)

*To what extent do they help to justify religious language?*

The philosopher **R. B. Braithwaite** takes a different line altogether in attempting to show the meaning of religious language. Unlike Wisdom or Hick, he is not interested in the possible truth of religious claims, because as an empiricist he does not think that they can be verified. He argues instead that religious assertions, while non-cognitive, are meaningful because they indicate a *way of life*, and can therefore be verified in terms of a person's behaviour and attitudes. Christian beliefs include beliefs such as 'God is love'. Such beliefs can be verified by the *effect* that they have in a believer's life. So, to say that God is love, argues Braithwaite, is to express the intention to live 'an agapeistic [loving] way of life'. Stories from the gospels can be understood as providing an incentive to do this. In his attempt to give meaning to religious language, Braithwaite makes a typical appeal to *empirical* effects (intentions and actions). This empiricist approach is not necessarily reductionist, but it deliberately stops short at visible effects. It rules out any consideration of a spiritual basis for religious language, since such a basis is presumed to be unknowable because it is unverifiable.

We can conclude this section by noting that the challenge of logical positivism has had the salutary effect of at least making believers aware of the problems of religious assertions. But has it shown that such assertions are meaningless? Within its own terms, the answer is a foregone conclusion. If 'meaningful' is already defined as only that which can be empirically verified or falsified, then religious language is automatically ruled out. This has led many to point out the irony of the verification principle itself. Since there is no sense experience by which it can be verified, it is either a tautology or a statement of metaphysics! In either case it is non-cognitive, and therefore meaningless. Hence the verification principle contained from the start the seeds of its own destruction!

Most people would, in any case, question the restriction of meaning to what can be empirically and experimentally verified. As the above parables show, personal beliefs and language about them can be meaningful (a) if they are consistent with facts about the world, (b) if there is no logical contradiction in holding the belief and (c) if some allowance is made for human trust. After all, it is not uncommon for people to hold beliefs that they know cannot be fully verified, at least in the interim. In everyday life people are happy to trust that many of their convictions, religious or otherwise (and the language they use to express them), are not only meaningful but are also true. In the final analysis, the verification principle failed because it was unable to cater for the complexities of human experience, and the peculiarly personal dimensions of language.

## Some key phrases in religious language

| | |
|---|---|
| Faith leads to understanding | Augustine |
| Faith is absurd | Tertullian |
| God must exist | Anselm |
| Reason is a foundation of faith | Aquinas |
| Faith is trust | Luther |
| Reason is corrupt | Luther |
| Faith is a wager | Pascal |
| Faith is a leap | Kierkegaard |
| God is given in the categorical imperative | Kant |
| God is perceived in the sense of absolute dependence | Schleiermacher |
| God is in the numinous | Otto |
| God is a Thou | Buber |
| God is ground of our being | Tillich |
| God is our ultimate concern | Tillich |
| God answers our transcendence | Rahner |
| God answers our infinite openness | Pannenberg |

*According to logical positivists, these phrases are meaningless. Are they?*

## The roots of religious language: the mystical

We have seen how some philosophers have responded to the verificationist definition of meaning, and the challenge to the meaningfulness of religious language. They have pointed to the fact that the world is open to different interpretations, and that religious believers are entitled to hold that the religious one is as valid as any other. Coupled with this is the fact that religious people are happy to hold their beliefs in the understanding that one day they will be confirmed as true. But is this going far enough? Many people would want to argue that religious language must have firmer foundations than this. A more promising response to the empirist challenge, they believe, is to expose the *roots* of talk about God, to show that the language of religion gives voice to a legitimate area of human awareness. In this way, it would be possible to plot the 'logical geography' of religious language. How does talk about God begin? Where does it come from? What gives it meaning? These are questions about the possible roots of religious language. Are there areas of human experience that can only be spoken about through the language of religion? As we saw in Chapter 3, the believer would want to insist that the answer is 'yes'. For Kant, the experience of moral duty (see Chapter 1) led to an awareness of God. For Schleiermacher, it was the deep sense of 'absolute dependence' that contains the roots of religious awareness, out of which is constructed the whole edifice of religious language. For Rudolf Otto, it was the sense of the numinous that underlay all religious awareness, and all subsequent expressions of it. **Keith Ward**, in *Holding Fast to God* (1982), sees talk about God as rooted in our awareness of the *human* dimensions of our experience:

> *We start talking about God when we start adopting a basic reactive attitude to all our experience, an attitude of response to it as expressive of moral purpose. 'God' is that mysterious depth which is mediated in certain symbols and events in our lives ... which is focally expressed in the images built up within religious traditions. That is the root of the theistic attitude ...*

## Ludwig Wittgenstein (1889–1951)

Ironically, it was not only theologians who called attention to the fact that some areas of experience were difficult to put into words. A study of the deeper roots of language, and the difficulties of expressing some areas of experience, would form a major theme in the later thought of the father of logical positivism itself, Ludwig Wittgenstein.

One of the most remarkable philosophers of the century, Wittgenstein was born in Vienna but moved to England in 1908 to study engineering. His interest in mathematics brought him to Cambridge, where he came under the influence of **Bertrand Russell** (1872–1970). He would later become professor of philosophy at Cambridge in 1930, but in 1921 he published *The Tractatus Logico-Philosophicus*, which was to become the

# God and Language

Wittgenstein did much to undermine the original force of logical positivism's critique of religious language

bible of logical positivism. It ruled out religious and ethical language as meaningless. Wittgenstein's famous saying of this period was 'Whereof one cannot speak, thereof one must be silent.'

## Language games

In later life, Wittgenstein underwent a change of opinion about the nature of language, which he expressed in *Philosophical Investigations* (1951). He moved from seeing language as a mirror of the world to seeing it as an expression of life. Language was about *use*. 'The meaning of any statement is given in the way in which it is used', he said. People *used* language in different ways and for different purposes. Language was for commanding, philosophising, investigating, theorising and story-telling. There was the language of poetry, drama, ethics, science, philosophy, religion and so on. The new slogan became 'Don't ask for the meaning – ask for the use.' It is said that this truth about language dawned on Wittgenstein while he was watching a football match. It occurred to him that there were different *language games* just as there are different ball games. A particular form of language reflected a particular *form of life*. We can apply this insight to the language game called religion. Religious language could now claim to be meaningful within the religious form of life.

## A SAD NATIVITY

Caravaggio's Palermo Nativity, stolen from Chiesa di San Lorenzo, Palermo, Sicily

> The Christian 'form of life' underlying its religious language is well brought out in this account of Caravaggio's superb painting:
>
> *Caravaggio's dark Nativity from Palermo is a Christmas picture with the saddest of stories to tell. This is a nativity that could almost be a pieta. What all the assembled are feeling, what has, if you like, stilled all their joy, is their shared foreknowledge of the infant Jesus' future. Here is a Jesus born to be a saviour through his own death on the cross. And everyone in the picture knows it. The painter knows it too, and is trying to express the tragic implications of the situation by comparing various kinds of human and pictorial darkness.*
>
> *It would not do at all if all nativities were like this one. All births end in death. But that should not invalidate the sweet and simple opportunity for celebration that most other artists have seized. There is, nevertheless, a dark truthfulness to Caravaggio's reading of the situation, inspired surely by his own confused awareness of the proximity of death.*
>
> Waldemar Januszczak

But the problem of verification remained, and how the language and thought patterns of religion could be justified to those who questioned them. Wittgenstein devoted a lot of thought to the question of what religion was about, and what the roots of religious language might be. He believed that it came from a region of experience which he called the *mystical*. As he put it, 'There are indeed things that cannot be put into words. They *make themselves manifest*. They are what is mystical.' The mystical belongs to the deepest level of our interaction with the world, which Wittgenstein said was 'unutterable'. Examples that he gives to illustrate this include the aroma of coffee, the experience aroused by music and deep human feelings of nostalgia. Wittgenstein, significantly, also included in the mystical the profound sense that people sometimes have of the sheer fact of the world's existence. As he once famously said, 'Not how the world is, is the mystical, but that it is.' As **Fergus Kerr** pointed out, in *Theology after Wittgenstein* (1989), Wittgenstein had a life-long interest in religion. He knew that when believers asked questions such as 'Why are we here?' or 'Why could this happen?', they were not looking for *causal* explanations. These are the explanations that science is able to provide. With the mystical, it is different.

The *Modern Catholic Encyclopedia* (1994) appears to confirm some of Wittgenstein's insights. It states that religious language is non-cognitive in the empirical sense, because it belongs more properly to the realm of feelings, conscience and decision. However, it says that 'the question for theology is how to integrate religion with our cognitive knowledge of the world'.

## The world

Not how the world is, is the mystical, but that it is – Wittgenstein

*How does this statement compare with Russell's (p. 32)? Is it philosophically significant?*

## Religion as cognitive

However, **James Richmond** argues that the term *cognitive* has been unfairly hijacked by logical positivism, which has already decided what should count as 'reality'. If 'cognitive' means knowledge about reality in the fullest sense, then religious language can claim to be cognitive. As he forcefully puts it:

> *The theologian should make it clear that there is a 'world' of religious, moral and existential experience, that moral demands, existential decisions and historical events are 'factual', that the dimensions of value, revelation and history are 'real', and that the religious, moral, existential and historical approaches to things are 'cognitive', yielding knowledge of 'reality'.*

# Language

**Empirical**
Limits what can be said to what can be verified by observation and experience. Claims that the language of science is the only true language

**Religious**
Uses empirical language to refer to things beyond the range of empirical verification. Claims to refer to legitimate areas of human existence, such as the moral, the aesthetic and the religious

*Can religious language claim to be cognitive, or possibly cognitive? How relevant is Pascal's wager to this question?*

Wittgenstein indeed helped to restore some respectability to religious language, but many of the problems about how exactly its meaning could be specified continued to engage theologians. Many decided that a new way of thinking about God might pave the way for a new way of expressing truths about Him that would make more sense to 'modern man'. To these ideas we now turn.

### THE UNSPEAKABLE

In his book *The Truce* (1963), Primo Levi, one of the Holocaust's greatest chroniclers, perhaps gave another reason for silence than Wittgenstein's, in his description of the tragic Hurbinek, a nameless child of Auschwitz. Maybe the child couldn't speak because, unlike us in our ordered world, and with our subtle academic distinctions about what is meaningful and what is not, nothing in his world had any meaning – nothing:

*Hurbinek was a nobody, a child of death, a child of Auschwitz. He looked about three years old, no one knew anything of him, he could*

> *not speak and he had no name; that curious name, Hurbinek, had been given to him by us, perhaps by one of the women who had interpreted with those syllables one of the inarticulate sounds that the baby let out now and again ...*
>
> *... After a week, Henek announced seriously, but without a shadow of selfconsciousness, that Hurbinek 'could say a word'. What word? He did not know, a difficult word, not Hungarian: something like 'mass-klo', 'matisklo'. During the night we listened carefully: it was true, from Hurbinek's corner there occasionally came a sound, a word ...*
>
> Hurbinek continued in his stubborn experiments for as long as he lived. In the following days everybody listened to him in silence, anxious to understand, and among us there were speakers of all the languages of Europe; but Hurbinek's word remained secret. No, it was certainly not a message, it was not a revelation; perhaps it was his name, if it had ever fallen to his lot to be given a name; ...
>
> Hurbinek, who was three years old and perhaps had been born in Auschwitz and had never seen a tree; Hurbinek, who had fought like a man, to the last breath, to gain his entry into the world of men, from which a bestial power had excluded him; Hurbinek, the nameless, whose tiny forearm – even his – bore the tattoo of Auschwitz; Hurbinek died in the first days of March 1945, free but not redeemed. Nothing remains of him: he bears witness through these words of mine.

## III NEW IDEAS OF GOD

In his highly influential and controversial book *Honest to God* (1963), the then Bishop of Woolwich, **John A. T. Robinson**, questioned the whole theistic tradition in which God was perceived as a supernatural being somewhere 'out there' or 'up there'. He believed that this way of thinking about God had become outdated. A new language for speaking about God was needed which (a) would make more sense to modern thinkers and believers and (b) would more effectively express the true nature and meaning of God. He puts it like this:

## God and Language

> *Traditional Christian theology has been based upon the proofs for the existence of God ... They argue from something which everyone admits exists (the world) to a Being beyond it who could or could not be there ... Now such an entity, even if it could be proved beyond dispute, would not be God: it would merely be another piece of existence ... Rather, we must start the other way round. God is, by definition, ultimate reality. And one cannot argue whether ultimate reality exists. One can only ask what ultimate reality is like – whether, for instance, in the last analysis what lies at the heart of things and governs their working is to be described in personal or impersonal categories.*

From this passage we get a good idea of the way in which the bishop would like to think about God. Instead of thinking of God as an independent Being, he thinks that it makes more sense to think of God in terms of 'that which matters most' in my existence. However, this idea is not new. It was already contained in the biblical distinction between the true God and *idolatry* – making a finite thing 'matter most' in one's life. The *moral* idea that God must have first place in one's allegiance was already spelled out in *existential terms* in the Ten Commandments. This has led thinkers such as **Karl Rahner** to argue that living according to one's lights is *existentially* equivalent to believing in God, no matter what personal religious or non-religious label a person may wear, whether they be believer or atheist. The second problem with the above passage is what looks like a logical jump from existence to essence. This is when the bishop asks whether ultimate reality is personal or impersonal. Here he comes remarkably close to incurring his own ban against identifying God as an objective Being. If ultimate reality is personal, it must have some objective status; otherwise it is merely an abstraction, like reality itself. Besides, to speak of ultimate reality as impersonal seems a contradiction in terms.

The bishop clearly intended to replace the old way of thinking about God with a new way, one that did not involve thinking of God as an objectified being above and beyond the world. Instead, he wanted to stress the notion that God – properly understood – must evoke a personal, existential response from the believer. Whether this involves, of necessity, having to give up belief in God's independent transcendent reality, as traditionally understood, is highly questionable. The shift to a more internalised God, located in the subjective consciousness, will become a major feature of some strands of modern theological thought. This will become apparent as we look at some of the more prominent representative influences in modern theology, many of whom form the background to the bishop's own thinking.

## Rudolf Bultmann (1884–1976)

One of the most influential theologians of the past 50 years, Rudolf Bultmann was first and foremost a New Testament scholar, a subject which he expounded with great distinction while professor at Marburg from 1921 to 1951. It was there that he came under the influence of the existentialist philosopher **Martin Heidegger** (1899–1976), whose penetrating if obscurely expressed analysis of human nature he adopted as the key to understanding the message of the gospel. To clear the way for a new understanding of the Christian message, Bultmann believed it was necessary to remove what he perceived to be the 'mythical' garments in which the story of salvation was clothed. In this endeavour, Bultmann showed a post-Nietzschean concern to rescue faith from the challenge of modern science, which had led to the 'death of God'. If the unscientific and mythical world view of the scriptures could be reinterpreted, the light of the Christian message of salvation might be allowed to shine through. Quite simply, a world perceived as flat, with the heavens above and hell below, a world populated by supernatural forces which cause miracles to happen, was seen by Bultmann to have lost its credibility in the scientific age. Tragically, as he saw it, the baby of religious faith was in danger of being thrown out with the bath-water of an outmoded science. But more significantly, he thought, there was a mistaken emphasis on the *objectification* of God, and His action in the world. Religious faith had come too close to being presented in terms more associated with the world of science. There was an unhealthy concern with facts, truths, historical accuracy, details about what really happened and so on. In the midst of all this, the real meaning of religious faith was being lost. Even God was being objectified, seen as another actor in a drama involving human beings. This is what Bultmann meant by myth. 'Myth is that manner of representation in which the unworldly and divine appears as the worldly and human', he said. Myth is any account or story in which God is acting in a manner similar to a human being. While this raises the question as to how else God, or God's action, could be spoken about if not in terms of (or by analogy with) human action, Bultmann believed that the objectification of God in the Bible simply obscured the essential message that it was trying to convey. And what is this message? Here Bultmann borrows from Heidegger.

Heidegger believed that the central figure of history is man, whose being cannot be objectified as if he was a *thing*. Man's essential nature is to *exist*, and existence is not a thing either, since it is not fixed or static. To exist is not to know, but to *will*. To exist in the full human sense is to realise one's potentialities. Bultmann could see immediately that Heidegger's philosophical analysis of what it means to be human could provide a key to understanding the Christian message of salvation. To be *saved* is to *exist* in the fullest sense; that is, to exist authentically. To speak of God (acting through Christ) is to speak of a new possibility of existing. Heidegger had also provided the language with which to speak about sin. Man is essentially *fallen*, and always finds himself in a situation not of his making (his *facticity*, as Heidegger called it). These facts give urgency to the task of existing authentically and realising one's full potentiality in life. For Bultmann, the inspiration to do so comes from God. That is the message of the Cross and the Resurrection. For Bultmann, therefore, God is the power, or the Spirit, who enables man to achieve authentic existence in the midst of the world.

Three important criticisms of Bultmann can be singled out. One is that he shows too little interest in the historical basis of Christianity (see Pannenberg, Chapter 3). All he seems to be concerned about is the existential implications of the gospel message. Secondly, his approach to faith comes across as rather dour and serious, if not depressing. It is difficult not to get the impression that a life not lived authentically is somehow wasted. Little room seems to be left for God's forgiveness of the prodigal or the wayward. Thirdly, his approach to God seems exceptionally individualistic. Under the influence of Heidegger, he seems to assume that life within any kind of community framework risks contamination by the 'crowd', and is bound to lead to inauthentic existence. Although he borrows much from the thought of St Paul, he does not do justice to something that is central to Pauline thought. This is the notion that Christianity is a communal religion. The Body of Christ is a crowd, not an individual (see Eph. 4.11–32). This fairly basic fact is a key feature in the reality of religion. People become, and to an extent remain, religious on the strength of the influence of those around them. The lonely individual, so prominent in existentialism, is not the ideal, or indeed normal, paradigm of the human condition.

Yet, in spite of these criticisms, Bultmann made an important contribution to showing how faith can and should be relevant to human existence. By demonstrating that faith in one respect was more a matter of the practical will than of the speculative intellect, and in another respect was fundamentally a solution to the problems of living in the world, he made an important attempt to make the idea of God relevant in an atheistic age. We can see many of his ideas echoed in the thought of our next representative theologian, John Macquarrie.

## John Macquarrie

We mention John Macquarrie not because he is an original thinker in the mould of Bultmann, but because he has been similarly influenced by Heidegger and has played an important role in popularising existential thought in the English-speaking world. Macquarrie firmly rejects the traditional idea of God, which stressed transcendence and objectivity, and replaces it with an idea of God that is expressed in language borrowed largely from the thought of Heidegger. Thus God is not a 'being' or even a 'personal being'. This kind of thinking, he believes, is central to classical theism, and has led to a distortion in the understanding of God.

As Macquarrie puts it, in *Principles of Christian Theology* (1966):

> *The idea of God has undergone many changes in the course of its history. At the mythological level God was conceived as a being much like ourselves ... At the level of traditional theism anthropomorphic elements were toned down in the interests of transcendence, though God was still thought of as a person, but a strange metaphysical kind of person without a body ... he 'dwelt' metaphorically beyond the world, though he kept it running and intervened in its affairs when necessary. He was another being in addition to the beings in the world. But science has shown that the world can get along as a self-regulating entity and we do not need to posit some being beyond it. In any case such a being would not be ultimate, because we could still ask about his being. Contemporary theology is beginning to move out of the phase in which 'God' meant an exalted being beyond the world.*

Instead, Macquarrie proposes thinking of God as 'being', that which enables all existing things to 'be' and makes it possible for them to be 'beings'. At this point, Macquarrie has a difficulty. Heidegger had similarly distinguished between Being and beings, but he had not identified Being with God. To enable Macquarrie to do so, he has to call God 'holy being'. Here he reflects the influence of Bultmann (and indeed Tillich) who made God a focus of existential decision or 'concern'. For Macquarrie, God (being) cannot be a neutral concept (it must be a focus of commitment and worship) and because of this he has difficulty in allowing for the objective reality of God. In other words, he comes dangerously close to making God (being) dependent on man, who is the 'house' of being, the site where Being is recognised. As a result, his understanding of God as being appears to require 'beings' to make him manifest. This would mean reducing God in some way. Because Being enables beings to exist, or 'let-be', Macquarrie believes he has a new way of explaining how God as holy being, responsible for the 'letting-be' of all beings, is the Creator of all things. But once again it is difficult to see how God in this view (being) can have any reality apart from the beings of His creation. A God so dependent on His creation is a greatly reduced substitute for the God of classical theism. An illustration of this may be provided by the symbol that Maquarrie considered old-fashioned, namely light (see above). God as holy being needs beings in which He can subsist, in the way that light needs *objects* to witness to its reality. But light exists as a reality whether or not there are things to see.

While Macquarrie's overall proposal has a certain novelty and attraction, it is difficult to imagine how it could appeal to the ordinary person without a philosophical background. In any case, he seems to overlook the basic point made by Wittgenstein that the mystical can only be contained in the empirical. To go for an abstract concept such as Being as the symbol of God is to by-pass the traditional wisdom of thinking and talking of God as an individual *being*, but infinite. This way of thinking about God has lasted for a long time not because it is ideal or perfect but because it is practical. As **Joseph Runzo** (1993) put it, 'Faith involves the ultimate commitment that one has indeed confronted God (in himself), a divine reality that is independent of our human minds. And it is the experience and life of faith which bridges the abyss that separates us from an otherwise unavailable God.' This is Runzo's defence of a realist conception of God as opposed to the non-realist view suggested by Macquarrie, but held in an extreme form by **Don Cupitt** (see below).

The extent of Heidegger's influence in theology will also be apparent in the thought of our next theologian.

## Paul Tillich (1896–1965)

Generally regarded as one of the most important theologians of the twentieth century, Paul Tillich studied and taught in several German universities, before emigrating to America when Hitler came to power. One of the most formative influences in his life, it is said, was his reading of Nietzsche in the trenches of the First World War. From this he learned of the crisis in theology which Nietzsche had described as 'the death of God' (see Chapter 3). Tillich's subsequent life's work was dedicated to restoring the credibility of religious belief, in a sense bringing God back to life. His method has been called 'correlation', showing the connection between the truths of faith and the human problems of living in the world. As he said in his monumental *Systematic Theology* (1951–1963), 'theology involves an analysis of the human situation out of which existential questions arise, and is an answer to those questions'. With this understanding, Tillich sought to mediate between religious faith and the non-religious, secular, indeed atheistic, culture of his day.

One of Tillich's first concerns was to deal with the idea of God rejected by Nietzsche. This was the God who was dead, the objective, transcendent God of classical theism. In its place, Tillich proposed a new understanding of God as the source and ground of our existence. God is in fact not a separate 'being', but Being Itself. This is only a new way of saying that God is ultimate reality. God is the power behind our existence, the power that gives us the courage to exist in the world in the face of anxiety, fear and the certainty of death. In this way, Tillich's God is seen as the answer to the problems of human existence in the world. This was partly in reply to Feuerbach and his followers, who had argued that belief in God was the cause of man's alienation and search for meaning. But Tillich added an important proviso. The true God must be man's 'Ultimate Concern', meaning that He must be the focus of man's highest values – one might even say 'that than which nothing can matter more'. He cannot be confused with any temporal or worldly concern, such as wealth, happiness or power. In time, these become transparently lacking in their capacity to satisfy man's existential needs. Thus Tillich's God is found in the depths of our existence, enabling us to be, and to realise our full powers to exist. For Tillich, the focal point of God's power in the world is the person of Jesus Christ. The whole language of the Christian faith is a symbolic system, bringing to expression the meaning of God for human life in community with others. Another radical approach to the understanding of God is proposed by our next thinker, Dietrich Bonhoeffer.

## Views of God

| Metaphysical | Existential |
|---|---|
| God is a supernatural being who is transcendent over man and is infinite, eternal, omnipotent and omniscient – classical theism | God is the answer to our existence (Kierkegaard), the solution to our moral awareness (Kant), the source of our dependence (Schleiermacher), the ground of our being (Tillich), the fulfilment of our transcendence (Rahner) |

*What is the danger of isolating one view from the other?*

## Dietrich Bonhoeffer (1906–1945)

Theologian and pastor until his death at the hands of the Nazis for opposing Hitler, Dietrich Bonhoeffer continues to be one of the most provocative voices within Christian theology. His call for 'religionless' faith puts him firmly in the post-Feuerbachian and post-Nietzschean tradition of trying to restore the credibility of God in the face of modern atheism. The outstanding theme in his thought is the necessity of embracing the realities of the secular, non-religious culture of our time. For Bonhoeffer, it is in the midst of our godless culture of today that the true God is to be found. The corollary of this is that the traditional Church has obscured the true nature of God by making man too dependent on supernatural assistance. A return to the scriptures is the key to understanding the logic of the apparent absence of God from human affairs. God is not necessarily found in 'religious' institutions such as the Church, but can be just as easily found in places that we least suspect. That is the message of the Cross. If God was in Christ who lived in the midst of his world, he can now be found in the midst of *our* world, in spite of all its godlessness. So Bonhoeffer could speak of the 'weakness' of God, a paradoxical notion intended to explain the need to solve our own problems in an adult way, without waiting for divine intervention.

With this approach, Bonhoeffer attempts to neutralise the challenge of atheism, especially in the aftermath of the illusory and discredited problem-solving and comfort-giving god of Marx and Freud. He does this by showing a way to embrace theism that does not involve (a) accepting the 'religious' objectified and transcendent God of classical theology, (b) accepting the traditional trappings of established 'religion' or (c) losing our human autonomy in the midst of the scientific and secular world. This means living 'as if God is not there', taking responsibility for our own lives. As he says in one of his *Letters from Prison*, shortly before his death:

> *God allows himself to be edged out of the world, and that is exactly the way, the only way in which he can be with us and help us. Man's religiosity makes him look in his distress to the power of God in the world. The Bible however directs him to the powerlessness and suffering of God ... We may say that the world come of age was an abandonment of a false conception of God ...*

In these words, Bonhoeffer appears to come close to what Feuerbach had held, namely that God's powers were really man's powers. Bonhoeffer, however, unlike Feuerbach, does not deny God, and does not overlook the reality of God's *grace*, which is visible to faith in the person of Christ. The reality of God's helping grace is to be found in the midst of life, all life.

The reality of Bonhoeffer's own personal faith is shown in this poignant account written by the prison doctor who witnessed his execution at Flossenburg in 1945:

> *Through the half-open door in one room of the huts I saw Pastor Bonhoeffer, before taking off his prison garb, kneeling on the floor praying fervently to his God. I was deeply moved by the way this lovable man prayed, so devout and so certain that God heard his prayer. At the place of execution, he again said a short prayer and then climbed the steps to*

*the gallows, brave and composed. His death ensued after a few seconds. In almost fifty years that I worked as a doctor, I have hardly ever seen a man die so entirely submissive to the will of God.*

The rejection of the objectified transcendent God of classical theism, evident in the thought of Bultmann, Tillich and Bonhoeffer, has been taken a radical stage further in recent times by our next theologian, Don Cupitt.

## Don Cupitt

Don Cupitt is a fellow of Emmanuel College Cambridge, a founder of the *Sea of Faith* movement of non-realist theology and a priest of the Church of England. In the light of his radical theological ideas, if they can be called that, many wonder how he can continue to call himself a Christian, let alone an official of the Church. This is because he rejects one of the linchpins of Christian theology, the belief in the objective reality of God. It is not that he goes along with the logical positivist challenge that *talk* about God is non-cognitive, telling us nothing about what is real or true. He goes further than this in denying that God has any independent reality outside the human mind. In saying that God is a construct of the mind, and Christ the embodiment of disinterested love, Cupitt returns full circle to Feuerbach and effectively becomes his apostle. Any attempt to locate God outside the individual consciousness is to dilute the true religious sense. As he puts it plainly in *After God* (1997), 'God is the "religious ideal" – that is, a unifying symbol of our common values and of the goal of the religious life.' But, as **Joseph Runzo** says, if the reality of God is rejected, 'why be religious at all, why go beyond humanism?' Paradoxically, Cupitt continues to believe that religion of a humanistic kind is still important in a therapeutic kind of way. In language that would hardly endear him to the logical positivists, what he calls the 'Eye of God' trick is 'the trick of relating oneself to oneself via the universal, seeing oneself and one's expressed life as if through God's eyes. This is what remains valuable in the *idea of God*' (my emphasis). In a similar vein, he says: 'The old way of living *coram Deo* [as if before God] was valuably consciousness-raising and morally stabilising, and one may usefully continue to pray to God just as one may find oneself talking to and thinking of a dead person.'

In a climactic passage that contains the full flavour of his thought, he writes:

> *The few who truly wish to attain religious happiness will also continue to discover that the way to it is by dismantling, dissolving away the realistic doctrines of both God and the self, so that the two can be melted together. Admittedly the spiritual marriage is a deadly heresy; but it is also eternal happiness.*

It seems that Cupitt so radicalises the notion of God that he leaves behind no recognisable trace of traditional Christian theism, beyond the recognition of its traditional benefits. As Lewis Carroll might have put it, nothing remains of the Cheshire cat of traditional theism except its lingering smile!

In the final section, we look at another modern idea of God which also rejects traditional theism, process theology.

## Language about God

**Realist**
God is an objectively real being who has freely created and redeemed man. He is 'That than which nothing greater can be conceived' – Anselm

**Non-realist**
God is a concept used and understood within the religious form of life. The concept only has meaning in so far as it promotes man's sense of moral integrity – Cupitt

*To what extent does the non-realist view depend on the realist view?*

## Process theology

Process theology is a twentieth-century movement in theology which has its philosophical beginnings in the thought of **Alfred N. Whitehead** (1861–1947). In *Process and Reality* (1929), Whitehead argued that reality as we know it is not a static entity, but is always in a state of process and development, an idea that is consistent with the theory of evolution and the Big Bang cosmology. If this is the case, argued

Whitehead, the fundamental principle behind all reality, God, must also be in process. Whitehead saw the world in relation to God as being somewhat comparable to the way the body is related to the person. God needs the world as I need my body. So, he could say 'It is as true that God needs the world, as that the world needs God.'

Process theology, which was later developed from Whitehead's thought, is sometimes called *panentheism*, meaning God is *in* the world. It is distinguished from *pantheism*, which is the view that God and the world are the same. Whitehead's ideas were taken up and developed by theologians such as **Charles Hartshorne**, in *Man's Vision of God and the Logic of Theism* (1941) and **Schubert Ogden**, in *The Reality of God* (1966).

**Hartshorne** believes that the 'process' approach provides a more coherent way of thinking about God, more suited to the modern mind, that is imbued with scientific ways of thinking about reality. Traditional theism had stressed the static, unchanging and perfect nature of God's essence. This idea of God has now fallen victim to the rise of science and is the God who is pronounced dead. Science shows a picture of the world which operates on fixed scientific laws with no apparent need of such a God. **Ogden** believes that the 'death of God' theologians such as **Thomas Altiser** have over-reacted against the old idea of God, and have virtually dismissed the idea of God altogether. What is needed is a new way of thinking and speaking about God which will restore God to a new level of credibility.

To find this new way of thinking about God, all that is needed is to go back to the Bible. The picture of God that the Bible gives us bears no relation to classical theism. In the Bible, God is dynamic – not a static unchangeable essence. Far from being immutable, God is constantly interacting and changing in relation to people (as can be seen in the stories of Abraham, Moses and the prophets). Ogden believes in the appropriateness of modelling God on the concept of a *person*. Persons are characterised by change and becoming, not by static changelessness. Process theologians try to find a middle way between the transcendent God of classical theism and the personal, dynamic God of the Bible. So how do they solve the problem of giving God an apparent 'creature-like' status? To explain this they go back to Whitehead's distinction between God as He is in Himself, and God as He is in relation to the world. This is called the *bipolar* concept of God. The distinction is also expressed in terms of God's *existence* and His *actuality*; or His *primordial* and *conse-*

*quent* natures; or again His *abstract* and *concrete* modes of being. In this view, the traditional attributes of God are retained, but reinterpreted. God is no longer omnipotent in the traditional sense. His omnipotence now means that God is able to use all things, even evil, to bring forth good. However, he does this not by force, but by persuasion.

This understanding of omnipotence makes process theology an important resource in *theodicy* (see Chapter 2). Here God is seen as a party in the world's suffering. He is not detached from the world's suffering, nor does He intervene to stop it. Rather, God is involved in the suffering of the world, as man's 'fellow traveller' and fellow sufferer.

Here, however, we come to the main problem with process theology. It tends to stress the *impotence* and helplessness of God, putting Him almost at the mercy of human beings. This is undoubtedly an attractive idea, but one fraught with difficulties. It appears to reduce God almost to the level of another human being, as **Hans Schwarz** points out in *The Search for God* (1975). Traditional theism was especially concerned to preserve those attributes of God without which He could not be God and the object of human worship. Central to those was the attribute of omnipotence. This can only be surrendered at the high cost of making God less than God.

Yet at the level of the ordinary believer, the process view of God has a certain ring of truth about it. **Donald Neil**, in *God in Everything* (1984), sees process theology as a way of breaking down barriers to unbelief. Modern atheism, he believes, is partly at least a reaction to the remote, transcendent God of traditional theism, which many people have found unsatisfactory. Process theology, he finds, is an attractive way of thinking about God today for four reasons:

1  It is more *intellectually* satisfying than traditional theology, because it takes into account, and incorporates, the scientific discoveries about the world. It also allows for the uninterrupted operation of natural scientific laws. In this way, it sees the action of God through scientific laws, not through miraculous divine intervention.

2  It helps people better at the *religious* level by encouraging them to see an activity such as prayer as a preliminary to working with God to improve the world.

3 It is more acceptable at the *moral* level because it allows for personal autonomy, in place of the traditional attitude of obedient submission. God is not seen as a law-maker laying down rules from above, but more as a friend and companion, who encourages and inspires from within the world and at the level of human life in the way that Jesus did.

4 It is also more acceptable at the *existential* level of everyday personal living. Life, with all its ups and downs, is seen as a partnership with God.

The sense that God is involved, and present as man's fellow traveller, helps to counteract the *Angst* and sense of absurdity of modern life, expressed by writers such as **Jean-Paul Sartre**, **Albert Camus** and others. This sense of absurdity, it is argued, is partly an outcome of a false idea of God, like the one revealed by Sartre in *The Devil and the Good Lord*:

> *I supplicated, I demanded a sign, I sent messages to Heaven, no reply. Heaven ignored my very name. Each minute I wondered what could be in the eyes of God. Now I know the answer: nothing. God does not see me, God does not hear me, God does not know me ... I am going to tell you a colossal joke: God doesn't exist.*

In conclusion, we can say that for all its drawbacks, and for all the difficulties that process theology creates in being at odds with the principles of classical theism, many of its theological ideas about God are remarkably consonant with our understanding of experience and with the God of the scriptures.

## God

| Classical theism | Process theology |
|---|---|
| Immutable | Changeable |
| Perfect | Dynamic |
| Transcendent | Immanent |
| Judge | Companion |
| Mystery | Fellow sufferer |
| Law-giver | Persuader |
| Giver of grace | Helper |

*To what extent does process theology either succeed or fail to do justice to God as a worshipful being?*

### THE DEPERSONALISATION OF LANGUAGE

Criticising the scientific reductionism of language which leads to the elimination of the moral and personal, **Roger Scruton**, in *Modern Philosophy* (1994), put it like this:

*The machine which is established for the efficient production of Utopia has total licence to kill. Nothing is sacred, and its killings are not murders (for which persons alone could be liable) but 'liquidations'. With the depersonalisation of the world comes a disintegration of language ... By emptying language of every vestige of moral idea, we change the way in which the world is perceived. Those crucial words around which our aspirations congregate – words like 'liberty', 'truth', 'right', 'democracy', 'peace' – are either banished from the language, or used to mean both of two opposite things, as in Robespierre's invocation of the 'despotism of liberty', the communist slogan 'fight for peace', or Lenin's description of totalitarian government as 'democratic centralism'. When the murder of twelve million people [the kulaks] is described as 'the liquidation of a class', or of six million [the Jews] as the 'final solution of the Jewish question', all reference to the human reality is expunged from discourse. The terms are abstract, bureaucratic, almost without reference. Vocabulary, syntax, logic and style take on a new purpose which is neither to describe the world nor to interpret it ...*

# Answering Examination Questions

## Answer the question

The first rule in any examination is to *answer the question that is set*. One way of failing to do this is by not reading the question carefully enough before starting your answer. Another common mistake is to take one supposed key word from the question, assume that the question is vaguely about a particular area of the course and then proceed to say all you know about it.

This is well known in examiners' circles as the 'set answer'. A question comes up, say, on science and religion, and the candidate throws in all he or she knows about science and religion. This might include explaining the scientific method, the meaning of empiricism, the meaning of metaphysics, the criticisms of the logical positivists, the problems of the literal reading of the Bible, how science and religion complement, or conflict with, one another, what different authors have said, and so on. You are doing yourself a great disservice if you ignore what you are being asked to answer. All of these aspects will no doubt be the ingredients of a competent answer, but if you simply jumble them together they will not get you the required academic credit.

## The bricks and the house

To use an analogy: The elements that make up an intelligent answer are like a pile of bricks. The bricks may be seen as knowledge. A badly prepared pupil will probably make an untidy mess with the bricks. A better pupil will build a small house. The best pupils will build a better house. The secret is to remember that a good answer is a putting together, in a logically coherent sequence, of a selection of relevant material to make an argument to answer the question.

## Knowledge, understanding and evaluation

It is hard to improve on these three headings, that provide the main landmarks in examination answers.

**Knowledge** of the subject area is a prerequisite for answering any question. This is shown through a command of technical vocabulary, an awareness of key distinctions, reference to important sources and what relevant scholars have had to say. Some of these will overlap into understanding: for example, 'the problem of evil' has to do with theodicy, the nature and power of God, the different kinds of evil, Irenaeus, Augustine, Hick, Moltmann, free will, and so on.

The second stage is **understanding**. There will be some overlap with knowledge, but there will also be scope for showing awareness of problems and difficulties, and of the different attempts of scholars to deal with these. The skill required at this stage is sometimes called **analysis**, the ability to 'tease out' the problem. The understanding stage also provides important scope for giving **examples** to illustrate the more general nature of knowledge: for example, in a question about revelation it will be important to give examples of 'general' and 'special' revelation, or of 'propositional' and 'non-propositional' revelation, the problems arising from these, and so on.

The third stage is **evaluation**. This stage inevitably draws on the previous two. Without the requisite knowledge and understanding, it is impossible to properly evaluate, or *assess*. In this stage, the pupil shows the ability to make comparisons between views, and to be able to identify their respective strengths and weaknesses. Any personal opinion must relate to these, and not be a mere statement of what 'I think': for example, for a proper assessment, Aquinas' Five Ways would need to be considered both in relation to existing faith and in relation to critical philosophical objections. It is a commonly repeated complaint from examiners that candidates either ignore, or leave themselves insufficient time, for evaluation *even though it was clearly stated in the question*: for example, 'Assess the cosmological argument for God's existence' involves more than just giving an account of the argument.

## Basis and structure

There is an important principle at stake here. Academic questions are not a test of general knowledge. They are a test of a pupil's ability to show a range of skills to achieve an objective. These include the ability to:

- think logically

- identify the problems related to the question set

- show a command of the *vocabulary* relevant to the question area

- *select* relevant information to answer the question with reference to scholarly views

- be able to evaluate the competing issues involved in the question, and

- ideally, be able to offer a preference as to the most important issue

## Planning

An important procedural principle in an examination is to take a few minutes to read the questions carefully before deciding which ones you are going to answer. The key factor is how well prepared you are going to be for a particular question. An important guide here is to make sure that you are going to be able to *show what you know*. There is nothing worse than overlooking a question that you *could have done well in* if only you had realised it at the beginning. Related to this is the skill of *making knowledge relevant to an answer*. This is one of the more satisfying aspects of academic success. There is never only one way to deal with a question. An answer can be justified in a number of ways if sufficient thought is used. However, it is important to be prepared for the more obvious aspects of a question – so first things first, in terms of basic preparation for 'what is expected' of the candidate.

A few minutes planning your answer at the outset can be well spent. Start with a random 'brainstorming' of ideas, and then list the ideas in order of priority. This will help to ensure that you do not set off on the wrong track and miss the point of the question. A useful idea is to try to come full circle towards the end, finishing off with reference to where you began. This will show that you were not trying to evade the question.

## Questions about God

## Analysis of the question

A sensible way to start on a question is to analyse the wording. If a question comes across as vague and difficult to decode, *say so* – and *why you think so*. This already shows that you have critical ability. Then answer the question in the light of its shortcomings! Equally, be on the lookout for qualifying words such as 'assess', 'how fair?', 'main', 'only', 'merely', 'cannot', 'absolute', 'satisfactory', and so on: for example, 'Does religion provide a *satisfactory* answer to the challenges of science?' This will involve addressing the meaning of 'satisfactory', both from a scientist's and a believer's point of view, using philosophical, or existential, and theological considerations.

## Sample outline answers

*1. Is faith irrational?*
Define faith. *Fides quae. Fides qua.* Fiducia.
Define reason. Rationality. Irrationality.
Faith and reason. Different views on their relationship: Augustine, Anselm, Pascal, Aquinas, Luther, Kierkegaard, Barth, Pannenberg.
Relation to natural and revealed theology, and to general and special revelation.
The idea that faith *should* be irrational. Disputes about whether reason is corrupt or aided by grace.
God of the philosophers and God of the theologians. Are they different?
Modern challenges of positivism and logical positivism. The parables. Existential analysis by Bultmann etc. The distinction between faith being supported by reason, and faith being consistent with reason.
Is faith irrational? Depends on the starting point. Can be argued yes, no and 'to some extent'. This could also be start of the answer.
Related questions: faith and knowledge, faith and revelation, revelation and knowledge.

*2. Are miracles credible in a scientific age?*
Define 'miracles', 'credible' and 'scientific age'. Assumptions behind each word.
Miracles and 'wonder'. Events attributed to God.
Traditional view: Augustine, Aquinas. Hume's definition. Hume partly right if issue is empirical.

Logical possibility of miracles if God exists. Problems for science in light of quantum physics. Impossibility of disproving a miracle.
Nature a closed system. Habgood, Wiles, etc.
Modern view of miracles as 'seeing as'. Hick. Possible to integrate with scientific explanations. More in accord with life as system of natural causes. Sees God acting through human agency. Avoids accusation that God acts selectively. Habgood, Wiles, Polkinghorne.
Link with process theology and the problem of evil. Flew, Wiles, Neil. Danger of making God 'weak', or making miracles merely subjective. Disputed.
The credibility of miracles depends on how they are understood. Traditional view still credible for many. Recent attempts to reconcile miracles and science possibly invite the accusation that too much is conceded to science. Disputed. In the end there can be no conclusive proof that a miracle did or did not happen. Still seen as credible within religious form of life.

## 3. How convincing are Aquinas' Five Ways as proofs of the existence of God?

Brief but accurate account of Aquinas' Five Ways.
Not clear that Aquinas ever saw his Five Ways as proofs in the strict sense of compelling evidence for God's existence. More modest claim of showing the meaning of 'what believers call God'. Aquinas attempts to show that 'what believers call God' provides the answer to legitimate questions about reality.
Five Ways not in themselves a profile of *Christian* God (explain).
But they do spell out important aspects of God's nature as Prime Mover, First Cause, Necessary Being, Highest Value and Origin of signs of *telos* in world.
Cosmological argument of Aquinas backed up by Leibniz; teleological argument backed up by Paley and by modern versions of the argument (Richmond, Farrer, etc.).
Rational arguments of this category belonging to traditional natural theology seriously undermined by Hume and Kant (explain).
Five Ways contribute to 'cumulative argument' stated by Swinburne.
Five Ways add significantly to believers' critical understanding of God. Limited for unbelievers in light of criticisms of Hume and Kant.
Represent serious attempt to show that faith is consistent with reason, used in search for explanations of 'why there is something and not nothing' (Leibniz).

## 4. How far are claims of religious experience open to non-religious interpretations?

Definition of religious experience. Distinguish between direct and indirect. Biblical examples.

Conversions and mystical experience. Examples.

Ideas of James, Smart, Jung, and so on, showing positive benefits of such experience. Stress on empirical character test of recipients.

Criticisms of Feurbach and followers, especially Freud (give details).

Contribution of psychology in analysing mental structure of religious experience (dependence, guilt, etc.). Differences between Freud and Jung.

Contributions of Schleiermacher and Otto in relating religious experience to ordinary human experience. Possible reference to Wittgenstein and the mystical.

Principle of credulity (Swinburne) and authenticity (Bowker).

If God exists, no logical impossibility of his being experienced directly or indirectly.

Refer to historical claims about revelation. Also critical history of scepticism about claims to religious experience within Christian Church.

Non-religious interpretations not conclusive. They do not in the end rule out a religious explanation of experiences claimed by mystics, converts and various believers.


## 5. How convincing are the objections of logical positivists to the claims of religion?

Explain logical positivism and its ancestor positivism (Comte).

Influence of Wittgenstein on the Vienna Circle and the bias towards scientific empiricism.

Ayer's verification principle and Flew's falsification principle.

Implications for religious claims in religious language.

Replies of Wisdom, Mitchell, Hare and Hick (parables), and Braithwaite.

Wittgenstein's ideas on 'forms of life' and the 'mystical'.

Is non-falsification a strength or a weakness?

Significance of empirical grounding of religious claims. Refer to traditional arguments for God's existence, and modern approaches through existential analysis. Ideas of Rahner on transcendence. Richmond's ideas about areas of experience accounted for by religion, and not by science.

Objections of logical positivists biased towards scientific truth. Did help to show need for greater clarity in religious language, and more awareness of its symbolic character. Not conclusive in showing that religious language is meaningless.

## 6. How successful is the moral argument as a proof of God's existence?

Introduction to the moral argument, with reference to Paul's claim that God's law is 'written' on the heart. Reference to Aquinas' argument from value.

Best known formulation of the argument by Kant. Moral experience gives rise to three postulates (will, soul, God).

The need for God to guarantee the *summum bonum* (equation of virtue and happiness), which is not attainable in this life.

Not a rational argument in the strict sense. An argument of the practical reason. Kant 'put reason aside to make room for faith'.

Need to make sense of categorical imperative. Can man's moral transcendence end nowhere?

Does Kant overlook human weakness as result of the Fall?

Significance of objection that Kant assumed a *moral law*. Can it be answered in terms of reality of personal sense of duty – whatever that is in substance?

Argument supported by Newman and others. Voice of conscience as the voice of God has ring of truth. Alternative is to see moral sense as ultimately aimless and meaningless. Dostoyevsky: 'if God does not exist then everything is permitted'.

Moral argument not conclusive. Requires faith and trust. Transparent to believers, but its logic remains unconvincing to agnostics. Would Kant the rationalist understand?

## 7. The existence of evil disproves the existence of God. Discuss.

Explain problem of evil. Only a problem in relation to classical theism. Theodicy.

The inconsistent triad. Hume's restatement, 'the rock of atheism'.

Used by Flew to show that 'God loves us' is meaningless.

If miracles, why does God not intervene?

Distinguish moral and natural evil. The problem of suffering.

The Augustinian Theodicy. The Fall and human free will.

The Irenaean Theodicy. Man made in God's image but not likeness. Popularised by Hick and Swinburne. The need for trial and development through exposure to suffering. The theory of 'soul-making'.

Assessment of the theodicies. Too theoretical?

Objections of believers: Dostoyevsky's novel.

# Questions about God

Shift to *practical* theodicy: Where is God when people suffer? Wiesel, Moltmann.

The scandal of Auschwitz. Ideas of Bonhoeffer, process theology, and so on.

Existence of God not disproved by evil for believers. To atheists shows evidence of no loving God (Sartre, Camus). Evil remains a human mystery which can heighten sense of *Angst* and meaningless of life.

*8. Assess critically Christian responses to Darwin's theory of evolution.*

Outline Darwin's theory. Why the theory caused controversy for Christians.

Clear reference to Genesis and related beliefs about creation, and nature of man.

To what extent does theory conflict with Christian assumptions based on Bible?

Contrasting reactions of Wilberforce, Temple, and so on.

Significance of Darwin's *Descent of Man*. Threat to key beliefs.

The meaning of creationism. Why fundamentalist creationism developed. Fear of 'godless' implications of evolution. The Skopes Trial.

More liberal responses: Teilhard de Chardin, Ford, Stannard, Polkinghorne, and so on.

Christian responses varied, but united in holding on to Bible's religious message.

Creationists well meaning, but possibly pay too high a price for resisting science. Man not possible to reduce to product of nature (Kant, Rahner, Bultmann, etc.)

Reconciliation of evolution and Bible now well established in principle.

# Glossary

**absolute**  Unconditioned, free from limitations, not **contingent**. The term was applied by Hegel to refer to the highest reality, which he identified with spirit.

*a posteriori*  An argument based on, or *after*, **experience**; for example, the **teleological** argument.

*a priori*  An argument based on ideas prior to, or *before*, **experience**; for example, the **ontological** argument.

**agnosticism**  Literally from the Greek *a*, 'against', and *gnosis*, 'knowledge'; an agnostic holds that some things, such as God's existence, cannot be fully known.

**analogy**  A method used in religious language of applying to God qualities based on those valued within human **experience**; for example, goodness, love, wisdom, care, justice, and so on.

**analytical statement**  Used in association with linguistic analysis. 'Analysis' means 'pulling apart'. Statements of mathematics and explanations of words are analytical. An analytical statement is said to be significant but trivial, because it says nothing new.

*Angst*  An existential term that denotes a fundamental malaise or anxiety about existence in the light of man's awareness of his potentialities in the face of **finitude** and death.

**anthropology**  From the Greek *anthropos*, 'man'; the study of human behaviour and human nature.

**anthropomorphism**  From the Greek, meaning 'in human form'; in theology it means the tendency to speak of God in human terms – for example, when we call God *father*, or when we say God is *angry*.

## Questions about God

**anthropic principle**   A principle associated with the fact that the universe couldn't be understood without man being here to observe it.

**Aristotelianism**   A system of thinking about reality derived from Aristotle (384–322 BC), which gives priority to sense **experience** as the basis of all knowledge. It was highly influential in the thought of Thomas Aquinas (see **Thomism**), and can be contrasted with **Platonism**.

**asceticism**   From the Greek *ascesis*, 'training'; the practice of fasting and self-denial, which has been a common feature of Christianity since the time of Jesus. It is closely linked to **mysticism** through the 'mystic way', and is generally regarded by most writers as a condition of progress in the spiritual life.

**aseity**   From the Latin *a*, 'by', and *se*, 'itself'; God's capacity to exist necessarily, or by Himself.

**atheism**   From the Greek *a*, 'against', and *theos*, 'God'; the view that there is no God.

**Atonement**   Literally 'at-one-ment'; the **doctrine** that Christ by His death reconciled, or made one, man and God.

**autonomy**   From the Greek *auto*, 'self', and *nomos*, 'law'; the idea of being able to determine for oneself one's **beliefs** and values. It is associated with **liberalism** and **revisionism**.

**Being**   A concept used by some existentialist thinkers, such as Heidegger, to mean that which lies behind every particular being, and in which all beings participate. It may be compared with the way in which light may be distinguished from particular lights. Tillich defined God as 'Being Itself'.

**belief**   A state of mind in which confidence, trust or **faith** is placed in a person, idea or thing.

**blik**   A word used by R. M. Hare to denote a **belief** that cannot be shaken.

**Church**   The Christian organisation that sees itself as responsible for the message and the theology surrounding Jesus Christ, and as guardian of the Bible. Historically it has clarified **beliefs** about Christ in Creeds and Councils.

**classical theism**  A term identified with the philosophical analysis of God from medieval times. It defines God as real, timeless, eternal, infinite, omnipotent, omniscient and perfectly good. It has been challenged by **process theology** and **non-realist** forms of theism.

**cognitive statement**  From the Latin, meaning 'knowledgeable'; statements restricted by **logical positivists** to what can be **empirically** verified. Religious statements are alleged to be 'non-cognitive' because there is said to be no empirical test for their truth or falsity.

**contingent**  From the Latin, meaning 'to happen'; used to suggest something happening fortuitously or by circumstances. Events or beings in the world are said to be contingent, since they might not have happened. God is said to be a non-contingent, or necessary, **Being**.

**conversion**  An **experience** of the **supernatural** that results in a change of life towards the service of God.

**cosmological**  From the Greek *cosmos*, 'world' or 'universe'. The cosmological argument is based on facts about the world. Cosmology refers to the study of the universe.

**creationism**  The view that reality is **ultimately** explicable only in terms of a divine Creator. In modern usage, it denotes the view that Genesis should be taken literally as a description of how the world was created by God. In its more **liberal** sense, it is consistent with scientific views of the world.

**deism**  From the Latin *deus*, 'God'; the view that God created the world but left it to run according to its own laws. In deism, God does not interfere in the world.

**doctrine**  From the Latin, meaning 'to teach'; the official teachings of the first Councils of the **Church**. For Catholics, it refers to all official teachings of the Church to the present day.

**dualism**  From the Latin *duo*, 'two'; a system involving two principles or forces. One system of dualism divides reality into good and evil. Descartes divided reality into mind and matter (Cartesian dualism).

**empirical**  From the Greek, meaning 'to try' or 'trial'; refers to **experience** as opposed to reason. Empirical evidence is the evidence of experience obtained through experiment and observation, and is identified with the methods of **science**.

**empiricism**  The philosophical theory that all knowledge about the world must be based on **experience**. Its typical exponent is David Hume.

**Enlightenment, the**  A period from roughly 1650 to 1780, characterised by the rejection of authority in favour of reason. Often used as a simple term for the challenge to **religion** typified by Hume and Kant.

**epistemic**  From the Greek *episteme*, 'knowledge'; a so-called epistemic distance separates man and God.

**epistemology**  Theories of knowledge such as idealism and **empiricism**.

**eschatological verification**  From the Greek *eschaton*, 'the end time' or 'the after-life'; associated with the theory of John Hick that religious **beliefs** will be verified in the next life.

**essence**  From the Latin *esse*, 'to be'; that which makes something what it is. God's existence is said to be identical with his essence, or His essence is to exist. Existentialist thinkers have argued that man's essence is not fixed, but must be created or shaped by the manner of his existence.

**existentialism**  A continental movement in **philosophy** that analyses the meaning of human existence. It claims that the individual must create his or her own form of existence, and take responsibility for his or her lifestyle and **beliefs**. It is traceable to Kierkegaard, who stressed **personal** subjectivity as the key to human existence. It exerts a strong influence in philosophy and theology.

**experience**  From the Latin *ex per iri*, 'from going through'; that which is perceived through the senses rather than deduced from reason. It is associated with the approach to **religion** established first by Kant, and later by Schleiermacher and Otto. It is non-controversial when concerned with what is **empirical** and verifiable, but controversial when interpreted in terms of aesthetics, morality and religion.

**expressivism**   The view that religious **beliefs** are merely expressions of an individual's convictions, and do not necessarily relate to reality.

***ex nihilo***   From the Latin, meaning 'from nothing'; used in connection with the **belief** that the world was created from nothing by God.

**faith**   A conviction not necessarily based on **empirical** evidence, but considered not contrary to such evidence, and usually associated with religious **beliefs**. It is widely claimed to provide access to important truths about reality, and is often contrasted with proven certainty. It forms part of an important debate about its relation to reason.

**Fall, the**   The theological theory about the events surrounding Adam and Eve in Genesis 2–3. It refers to man's 'fall' from grace following Adam's disobedience, and is key to Paul's explanation of the Redemption by Christ in Romans 5.

**falsification**   Associated with the claim that religious **beliefs** cannot be proved wrong by **empirical** evidence. The reverse of **verification**.

**fideism**   The position that **faith** is immune to **rational** investigation, and can be internally justified; associated with Luther and Kierkegaard.

**fiducia**   From the Latin, meaning 'trust'; highlighted by Luther as the **essence** of **faith** being trust in God as opposed to assent to religious truths.

**finite**   From the Latin, meaning 'end'; the nature of the world and of man. It is contrasted with the nature of God as infinite.

**finitude**   a term used by existential writers to denote the human awareness of death. It is seen as a disturbing aspect of human life that contributes to ***Angst*** or anxiety. It has been used by Tillich and others to raise the question of God's existence.

**fundamentalism**   A term derived from a movement in America based on certain fundamentals about the Bible, such as the literal truth of the creation story of Genesis. It is identified with the view that the Bible should be interpreted literally, regardless of the findings of **science**. It regards the theory of evolution and other related scientific discoveries as **reductionist**   in nature, and as a threat to the status of man as the child of God. It is totally committed to preserving the spiritual values of the Bible.

**idealism**  So-called 'critical idealism' refers to Kant's distinction between what we are given in **experience** and the part played by the mind in making experience possible. In this view, not only is the mind a major element in how we come to know things, but we can only know what is first in experience. Thus **metaphysics**, and any attempt to know what lies outside experience (such as God), becomes impossible.

**illusion**  A **belief** that is seen as a source of comfort, which may be true or false. It should be distinguished from 'delusion', which is contrary to reality. Freud called **religion** an illusion, but believed it to be false.

**immanent**  From the Latin, meaning 'to dwell in'; the **belief** that God is not separate from the world, but is somehow in the world.

**ineffable**  From the Latin *effabilis*, 'speakable'; that which cannot be described in words. It is associated with claims of mystics, and people who claim that religious experiences defy verbal expression.

**language game**  A term used by Wittgenstein to show that language functions differently in different contexts; for example, physics, poetry, ethics and **religion**.

**liberal**  From the Latin, meaning 'free'; it refers to viewpoints that differ from traditional or conservative teachings, and is the opposite of **fundamentalism**. Liberal interpretations of scripture take into account the latest findings of scholars. So-called 'liberal theology' in nineteenth-century Germany followed Schleiermacher in basing religious knowledge on human **experience**, but was strongly rejected by Barth as being too humanistic.

**logical positivism**  A movement in **philosophy** based on positivist principles, that the only reality is the **empirical**, and therefore the only reality that can be spoken about.

**materialism**  The philosophical view that reality does not go beyond the material world, and that all living organisms, including human beings, are **ultimately** material substances.

**metaphysics** Theories about realities beyond the physical world – which were discredited by Kant as impossible, since we can supposedly only know about appearances. The term is closely linked to **natural theology**.

**miracle** From the Latin, meaning 'to wonder'; it traditionally meant an event caused by God which was contrary to the laws of nature, but it now has a wider meaning to include ordinary events seen as (indirect) evidence of divine intervention.

**mystery** From the Greek, meaning 'secret'; associated with the sense of the divine or holy spoken of by religious thinkers.

**mysticism** An alleged **experience** of oneness with God, as claimed by mystics.

**myth** An event that need not be understood to have happened as described, but which contains a deeper truth. The term is associated with Rudolf Bultmann, who saw a myth as any biblical event in which God is described in **anthropomorphic** (human) terms. To 'demythologise' is to extract the hidden (existential and religious) truth from the myth.

**naturalism** A philosophical view that reality does not go beyond the things and events of the natural world. It logically implies **atheism**.

**natural theology** Attempting to know about God by reason alone. The term is associated with **proofs** for God's existence.

**noetic** From the Greek, meaning 'mind' or 'intellect'; used in connection with **mysticism**, in the claim that the mystical **experience** is a source of knowledge.

**numinous** A term used to denote that which is beyond the **empirical**, but can still be an object of **experience**. It is sometimes used to describe that which is perceived to be mysterious, and is associated with the thought of Rudolf Otto.

**ontological** From the Greek *onta*, 'being'; having to do with being and reality. The ontological argument is an attempt to establish that God's being involves His existence.

## Questions about God

**pantheism**   From the Greek *pan* 'all', and *theos*, 'God'; the view that the world and God are identical – that God is all, or everything. It is associated with Spinoza.

**panentheism**   This differs from **pantheism** by seeing God in everything, (from the Greek prefix *en*, meaning 'in'), suggested perhaps by the way in which salt is in seawater. It is typical of the view, held by process theologians, that God is in the world.

**parable**   A story that illustrates a truth or a point.

**paradox**   An apparent contradiction. The term is associated with Kierkegaard, who used it to denote something almost impossible to understand, such as the idea of God becoming man.

**personal**   Having the characteristics of a person. It can be contrasted with an objective thing. In Buber's thought, the personal 'You' is contrasted with the impersonal 'It'. In Christian theology, God is seen as personal. The alternative to a personal cause of the world, it is argued, must be that of chance.

**phenomenology**   Rooted in the Greek *phainomenon*, 'to appear'; a philosophical system associated with Edmund Husserl, which attempts to describe human experiences as they appear to consciousness. It represents a reaction to the impersonal nature of **science**, which seeks to establish objective facts at the expense of how things appear to people in ordinary life as imbued with meaning. While science might describe a house, phenomenology would describe a home.

**philosophy**   From the Greek, meaning 'love of wisdom'; the search for truth in all its forms by using reason alone. What the subject matter of philosophy should be is itself a philosophical question.

**philosophical theology**   The study of the meaning and coherence of theological **beliefs** from a **rational** point of view.

**philosophy of religion**   The critical study of the foundations of religious **beliefs** from a philosophical point of view. It is associated with study and criticism of the arguments for God's existence.

**physicalism**  From the Greek *physis*, 'nature'; similar to **materialism** and **naturalism**, the view that the only reality is that which is physical.

**Platonism**  A system of thinking about reality, derived from Plato (417–347 BC), in which the world of sense **experience** is considered inferior to the world of Ideal Forms on which it is based. It has been influential in Christian thought since Augustine, and it has led to a disparagement of the material in favour of the spiritual.

**positivism**  A philosophical movement that rejects **metaphysics** and **religion**, claiming that the only true knowledge is that obtained by observation and **experience**.

**predicate**  In ordinary usage, that which is said about something – for example, 'An elephant is an animal'). It was disputed by Kant in his criticism of Anselm that 'existence' was a predicate, since a concept does not require that it actually exists – for example, elephants may be extinct. It has been counter-argued that existence is a necessary and defining predicate in the unique case of God.

**process theology**  A theological system based on the idea that reality is in process rather than being already fixed, and that God is acting within the process. It stresses God's **immanence** rather than His **transcendence**.

**proof**  **Empirical** evidence that something is true or false.

**psychology**  A system of thought based on a study of the working of the human psyche, particularly the unconscious. It is associated with Sigmund Freud, who pioneered the method of psychoanalysis, and has become linked with theories about the nature of **religion**.

**rational**  In accordance with reason. **Rationalism** is associated with thinkers such as Descartes, who held that certain ideas were innate (in-built) and did not depend on **experience** for their truth to be understood; for example, the truths of mathematics.

**rationalism**  The philosophical approach that gives priority to reason as the primary source of truth; in contrast to **experience**, which is seen as a less reliable source.

**realism/non-realism**  A modern term in theology related to the idea that God can be understood in either an objective (realist) or subjective (non-realist) way. Traditional theism saw God in a realist way, meaning that God was a **Being** with objective reality. Non-realism locates God in the subjective consciousness and appears to deny His objective reality.

**reductionism**  The practice of explaining events exclusively in terms of the natural or social sciences. A religious explanation is incompatible with an explanation that 'reduces' an event to a natural phenomenon, or a subjective **experience**. Explaining events in terms of natural phenomena – for example, in terms of psychological needs – does not necessarily involve reductionism.

**religion**  A word that is almost impossible to define; generally, a system of **belief** about the **supernatural**. Monotheistic religion such as Christianity focuses on belief in a supernatural **Being** called God.

**revelation**  A technical theological term meaning the disclosure by God of certain truths about His nature and will that are not accessible to reason. The precise nature of revelation is a matter of dispute.

**revealed theology**  The study of **beliefs** based on God's **revelation** of Himself in the Bible. It includes use of philosophical ideas to explain the significance of such beliefs and their coherence.

**revisionist**  A modern term used to denote controversial ideas that *revise*, or break away from, traditional ones. An example is the modern idea that God can be understood in a **non-realist** way.

**righteousness**  As applied to God, this means that He is always in the right. It is supposedly challenged by the existence of evil and suffering, and answered by **theodicy**.

**science**  From the Latin *scientia*, 'knowledge'; it has come to be identified with **empirical** knowledge. The so-called 'scientific method' refers to the obtaining of knowledge about the world through experimentation and **experience**. It is often contrasted with **religion** and **metaphysics**.

**secularisation**  From the Latin *saeculum*, 'an earthly time'. A modern *de facto* trend characterised by a non-religious view of the world. The supposedly modern 'secular age' is contrasted with the 'age of **faith**'.

**secularism**  An ideology that opposes religious influences, and attempts to replace **religion** with 'secular' or worldly ideas.

**supernaturalism**  From the Latin *super*, 'over' or 'above'; the **belief** in a **transcendent** God who exists above and beyond the material or physical world.

**symbol**  Something from the **empirical** world used as a key to refer to the **supernatural** world of religious **faith**. The Cross is the outstanding Christian symbol. Other realities such as light have been used as symbols to express truths about God.

**synthetic statement**  From the Greek, meaning 'bringing together'. Such statements bring together subject and **predicate** in such a way that they can be verified or **falsified**. Religious statements are alleged not to be properly synthetic.

**teleological**  From the Greek *telos*, an 'end' or 'goal'. The term has become identified with the notion of design or purpose. The teleological argument is based on the contention that the world exhibits evidence of design or purpose, and so points to God.

**theodicy**  From the Greek *theos*, 'God', and *dike*, 'justice'; the attempt to vindicate the goodness and justice of God in ordaining or allowing moral and natural evil and the human suffering that they cause.

**Thomism**  The system of thought derived from Thomas Aquinas. Under the influence of Aristotle, Aquinas attempted to throw light on the world of sense **experience**. This led to his conviction that the material world needs an explanation from beyond itself. The result was his Five Ways for proving God's existence.

**transcendence**  A quality belonging to human beings by which they are capable of going beyond their limitations, unlike the lower animals. It has been used by some thinkers to claim that only God can fulfil man's restless transcendence.

**transcendent**  From the Latin, meaning 'to go beyond'; associated with the claim that God is completely beyond the world and is totally different from man.

**Trinity** The Christian **belief** that God is three persons in one nature, Father, Son and Holy Spirit.

**ultimate** From the Latin, meaning 'last'; used in the context 'ultimate cause' or 'ultimate explanation'. From a theological point of view, God is the ultimate cause of the world. Non-believers deny the need for such a cause or explanation.

**verification** From the Latin *veritas*, 'truth'; associated with **empiricism**, to mean the process by which something can be shown to be true or false. According to **logical positivists**, religious statements are incapable of **empirical** verification and are therefore meaningless.

*via negativa* An aspect of the *via positiva*, it means qualifying all positive statements about God on the understanding that God is a **mystery** whose being cannot adequately be expressed in human language. In a sense, both ways go together.

*via positiva* The method of speaking about God that goes back to Pseudo-Dionysius. Typically, it is based on the highest human qualities, which are then applied to God in a pre-eminent way (hence the *via eminentiae*) – for example, God is perfectly wise, just, and so on.

# Index

agnosticism  68, 79
anthropic principle  35, 44, 59–60, 86, 87
atheism  37, 68, 103, 104, 120, 122, 131–132, 170
Augustine of Hippo  96–97
Auschwitz  110, 132, 157

Big Bang theory  24, 61, 62, 74, 75, 168–169
biology  51, 58, 61, 71, 75, 80, 83
bipolar concept  169–170

Cartesian Split  48
categorical imperative (Kant)  38–39
causality  28, 36, 78
conversion  94–98, 107
cosmological argument  28–29, 31–33, 36
cosmology  46, 61–63, 75, 77, 80, 83
creationism  see scientific creationism
cumulative case argument  43–44

Darwinism  see evolution, theory of (Darwin)
death of God (Nietzsche)  88, 123, 160, 164
dependence (Schleiermacher)  6, 92, 107

Descartes' triangle  25
designer, God as  33, 34, 36, 37, 50, 71, 74

Eckhardt, Meister  102–103
epistemic distance  129
evil, problem of  36–37, 125–134
evolution, theory of (Darwin)  34, 39, 52, 53–60, 71, 72, 75, 119, 168–169
Eye of God (Cupitt)  167

faith  6, 7, 10–16, 131–132
falsification  144–146
Five Ways (Aquinas)  1, 13, 29, 30–31, 112
fossil record  51–52, 67, 68, 75
free will defence  126–128
fundamentalism  63, 65–66, 69, 71

gap theory  67–68
geology  51, 75, 80
ground of our being (Tillich)  21, 88, 124

historical–critical method  5, 64, 65
history, science of  63–65, 83
Huxley–Wilberforce debate (1860)  57, 72

illusion, religion as  41, 118, 120
immanence  20–21, 74
imperative  *see* categorical imperative
Inconsistent Triad  125

language games  153–156
language, symbolic  139–141
*Laws* (Plato)  29
logical positivism  21, 106, 135, 143–144, 152, 167

*Meditations* (Descartes)  25, 26
miracles  109–111
moral argument (Kant)  37–40
Moses  89–90, 91
mystic way (St Bonadventure)  99
mystical experience (James)  100
mystical tradition  92, 99–103
mysticism  98–103, 105
myth  141–142, 160

natural selection  53, 75
nihilism  123

observation, empirical  47
Oedipus Complex  118
omnipotence  16–18
omniscience  18–19, 20, 127
ontological argument (Anselm)  23–28

Paley's watch  34–35, 50, 71,

Pascal's Wager  14–16
Paul of Tarsus  95
personal nature of God  22–23
process theology  168–171
*Proslogion* (Anselm)  23, 24, 26

quantum physics  80–82

reason (Descartes)  48, 106
Reformation, the  5, 10, 12, 41, 44
religious experience  89, 92–111
revelation  2, 5–10

scientific creationism  66–67
spheres (Teilhard de Chardin)  60
*Summa Theologica* (Aquinas)  30
*summum bonum*  39, 40

teleological argument  33–35, 36, 41, 44, 77
theodicy  125, 126–131, 170
theology  1–3, 8, 17–18, 19, 20, 21, 26, 35–37, 42, 44, 49–51, 63, 75–76, 168–171
time  19–20
transcendence  9, 20–22, 40, 74, 159, 160

verification  144–146, 149, 150
visions  89–90, 107

Wesley, John  97
world view, medieval  45–46